THE MID-ATLANTIC COMPANION

DAVID FROST &
MICHAEL SHEA

THE MID-ATLANTIC
COMPANION

or

How to Misunderstand Americans
as Much as They Misunderstand Us

Illustrations by Bud Handelsman

WEIDENFELD AND NICOLSON
LONDON

To Carina, Mona, Katriona, Ingeborg,
Miles and Wilfred,
without whose love and affection
we would have written the book in half the time

First published in Great Britain by
George Weidenfeld & Nicolson Limited
91 Clapham High Street, London SW4 7TA
1986

ISBN 0 297 78703 9

Printed and bound in Great Britain by
Butler & Tanner Limited, Frome and London

Contents

Acknowledgements

This book would not have been possible without the twinkling assistance of Fred Metcalf, who acted as the authors' sounding board and was a constant source of additional ideas. Our views on the American side of the Atlantic were monitored, focused and enhanced by Barbara Lippert and Clare Clifton. Many conversations with friends were of inestimable value, among them Peter Hickey, Ben Ramos, John Haslam, Edward Adeane, Jim Lizius, Adam Wise, Ken Johnston, Norman Lornie, Giles Gordon, Michael Shaw and Clay Felker. The words of Michael Shea appear by kind permission of Sarah Brennan. The words of David Frost appear by kind permission of Tricia Pombo. Their time, patience and typewriters were as ever invaluable.

Foreword

If you are one of those world-weary travellers addled, befuddled or simply inebriated by a mix of jet-setting hospitality and experience, one who is – or lets us believe he is – at home in every major world capital, lay down this book. It is not for you. If, however, you are not averse to having your prejudices catered to or indeed polished up as regards the odd little ways (some of them very odd and very little) and lifestyles (often dangerously different) that you are going to encounter on the other side of the Atlantic, then some of the misconceptions and confusions laid out in the following pages may not come amiss.

In this age of supersonic travel, to some the Atlantic is little more than a river – or a swamp. Sure, a myriad of things are exactly the same on both banks, like apple pie... well, perhaps not that either. But attitudes in Britain and the United States, despite, or perhaps because of, the television image of each as presented to the other, can in reality be radically different. The two nations are not two nations: each is several. British and Americans are separated by many more things than just a common language, with even that common language commonly uncommon. We are as biased, even bigoted, about each other as we are prejudiced in favour of ourselves. We have different obsessions, laugh at different things, play different games, eat different things in different ways (note the peculiarly American delight in mixing totally incompatible flavours on the same plate) and worship at many different altars. So many surprising and commonplace things are, well, different 'over there'. Thus the story of the bemused American who thought he had condemned to the scrapheap of fiction rumours of supposed British reticence when, driving through the West Country, he saw a van with the words 'Maidenhead Removals' on its side is matched by tales of British travellers who admire the American economy of effort in managing to do with one finger what has always taken the British two.

When we sat down to prepare this book, we were much encouraged by the words of James T. Farrell when he said, 'America is so vast that almost everything said about it is likely to be true, and the opposite is probably equally true.' Given our steadfast belief that indecision is the key to flexibility, this seemed to give us a clear run on anything we might write about the United States. Unfortunately we could not find a similar absolution for the British end of the book, but that has not prevented us from being governed by a policy of benevolent irresponsibility.

Having dipped into so many guidebooks, most of which claim to be indispensable, we have, by contrast, decided to offer you the first totally dispensable guidebook to help you on your way. We do not guarantee the relevance of any of our comments, the validity of any of our opinions, nor indeed the wisdom of any of our conclusions. Our simple hope is that, as you sit waiting for your plane in some crowded departure lounge, one of those antechambers of the skies (or whatever), you will enjoy thumbing through the pages of this book as much as we have enjoyed preparing them, and that whenever your next journey comes along, the Mid-Atlantic may prove as companionable to you as it has been to us.

David Frost
Michael Shea

1
Rumour and Reality

An asylum for the sane would be empty in America.

GEORGE BERNARD SHAW

A soggy little island huffing and puffing to keep up with Western Europe.

JOHN UPDIKE

Your newspapers are too big, and your lavatory paper's too small.

ERNEST BEVIN

There'll always be an England, even if it's in Hollywood.

BOB HOPE

I begin to think that America *is* an entertainment industry.

RUSSELL DAVIES

THE RUMOUR

To begin at the beginning (a well-established practice to follow), let each reader shed his preconceived ideas, cast aside morsels of hearsay, bypass second-hand bigotry and abandon pre-selected items of conventional xenophobic wisdom. All is not what it seems on the other side of the Atlantic. But before leaving such inherited prejudices entirely, let us identify them briefly so that we recognize them for what they are. One never knows: some may even be retained and developed for future use.

THE TRADITIONAL BRITISH VIEW
OF AMERICA

Most Americans are, in terms of traditional British caricature, brash, camera-slung, loud-mouthed, overdressed, overpaid ('... oversexed and over here', as they said about the GIs), naïve and, above all, over-familiar and lacking any of those pre-eminent British qualities of reserve and restraint. There is a widespread view, borne out by Michael Shea's experience on his first transatlantic crossing, that any American will, shortly after introducing himself (no refusals), tell you in detail all about his wives, mistresses, illegitimate children, brushes with the law, shrinks and tax problems. Nothing is sacred (except his salary); not even his politics, of which more later. They seem incapable of holding back awhile, keeping it secret, letting it out slowly.

One thing not to worry about, incidentally, is latent anti-Americanism in Britain; it will never rival anti-Americanism in America. Basically that is because, at root, Brits find Americans hard to dislike. Unlike the French, for instance, Americans generally have the decency to try to speak the same language even if, to quote one disgusted elderly Brigadier from Tunbridge Wells, they can't actually speak decent Shakespearean English.

Ladies and gentlemen, we are starting our descent to New York. It's a horrid place, but the **real** America is even worse.

The traditional British view of America can thus be summarized symbolically as follows: $$$, hamburgers, frankfurters, jeans, Coke, *Dallas*, Reagan, Mafia/bootlegging/speakeasies, whores with a heart of gold, wide-brimmed hats, tartan trousers, Kojak, chewing gum, Stars and Stripes, upside-down sergeants' stripes, Vietnam, *MASH*, Hollywood, surreys with fringes on top, badly behaved noisy children, Mickey Mouse, bald eagles, Fifth Avenue, shrinks, motels, Abraham Lincoln, string ties, cowboys and Indians, McDonald's, country and western music, Cadillacs, yellow cabs, millionaires, drive-ins, barbecued spare ribs, BLTs, diet anythings, blue-rinsed old ladies, very few blue-rinsed old men,* limos, Bermuda shorts, condominiums, neon, chocolate chip ice cream, JFK, the Em-

---

*They all killed themselves amassing money for the blue-rinsed old ladies.

pire State building, pancakes and syrup for breakfast, Mount Rushmore, Fred Astaire, gun-toting policemen, extra big everythings, the Statue of Liberty, those odd desert rock formations that appear in most Westerns, bigger and better everythings from Texas, and more $$$.

Sober Brits tend, with Eldridge Cleaver, to worry, fume, be dismayed or panic over the fact that it appears

> ... that the destiny of the entire human race depends on the outcome of what is going on in America today. This is a staggering reality to the rest of the world: they must feel like passengers in a supersonic jet liner who are forced to watch helplessly while a passle of drunks, hypes, freaks [and we might add: senile old men, hatchet-faced Pentagon generals] and madmen fight for the controls and the pilot's seat.

THE TRADITIONAL AMERICAN VIEW OF BRITAIN

By contrast – at least *not* by contrast – the American view of little old us is equally ... traditional. For example, first things first. They don't even get the name straight. They usually call the islands 'England'. Yes, of course they know that there is also Scotland. But that's different: mountains, tartan, whisky and golf. And Wales? Yes, that too: coal mines and song. And Ireland? Ah, yes: shamrocks, leprechauns and 'the Troubles'. There's certainly a tricky problem of definition here. We'll come to that later. They are amazed that the precise title of these offshore islands of Europe is the United Kingdom of Great Britain (the main island) and Northern Ireland, otherwise known as Ulster or the 'Six Counties', i.e., those stuck at the top of the island of Ireland that are not part of the Republic of Ireland. They don't even use the shorthand 'Britain' or 'the UK', which would do nicely. They don't realize that while the UK's capital (and England's) is London, Scotland has its own national capital, Edinburgh; Wales has Cardiff and Northern Ireland has Belfast. Their ignorance of the real Britain is matched only by Britons' ignorance of the real America.

Americans think of the British as living in a class-dominated, fogbound Dickensian museum, talking in admirably prim waspish ways, wearing formal clothes, driving Rolls-Royces, yet with a threadbare economy, a 'toothless bulldog' of a nation that 'has lost an Empire and has not yet found a role' (to quote that acerbic American Secretary of State Dean Acheson). Touch of truth all round, but they don't realize that this Hollywood-familiar, prissy upper crust comprises a tiny minority found only at a few socially established events and locations and projected mainly in the US of A by *Masterpiece Theater*-type epics produced by British television, on lines that have doubtful contemporary relevance. As for British currency, well they know that the pound sterling is currently just this side of monopoly money. (But this is somewhat more favourable than the American view of France, 'where you can't tear the toilet paper, but the money comes apart in your hands'.)

The traditional American view of Britain could thus be summarized symbolically as an amalgam of bangers (sausages), bobbies, beefeaters, Robert Morley, fog, cricket, Concorde, Alistair Cooke, *Masterpiece Theater*, James Bond, city gents in bowlers, Sherlock Holmes/deerstalkers/meerschaums/capes, Rolls-Royces, Jaguars, the upper class, the weather, Shakespeare, pubs, kilts, redcoats/tricorn hats, the Beatles, Churchill, Dickens, the Royal Family (all varieties), eccentrics (even more varieties), the Union Jack, butlers, warm beer, punks, the Cotswolds, the Tower of London, pearly queens, London cabs, Harrods, Boy George, Mrs Thatcher, Bath Olivers, bowlers, cider-swilling rustics, tripe and onions, and tea parties (Boston and other varieties).

AMERICAN PERCEPTIONS OF THEMSELVES

The United States knows that it holds the world together. It is the last bastion of democracy, human progress and liberty. With a little bit of help from its analysts, shrinks and social pundits, it knows it is living proof that the melting pot works, except where it doesn't, and, to quote Jimmy Carter in an unusual access of wit, ends up more like a bowl of warm minestrone. America (meaning for most Brits, only the United States) is the centre of everything, and thus Americans cannot understand why anyone seems to hate them. Everywhere else, godlessness prevails to a greater or lesser degree. Here anyone can get to the top. After all, look at some of those who have. Achievement is all. Thus Lily Tomlin: 'Ninety-eight per cent of the adults in this country are decent, hard-working, honest Americans. It's the other two per cent that get all the publicity. But then – we elected them.' They claim to have invented golf, tennis, hamburgers, frankfurters, chips (French fries), television, the telephone, computers, culture generally, the steam engine, Richard Burton, Elizabeth Taylor, Charlie Chaplin, the US Navy and Davy Crockett ... Ahem! Ahem! Wait a minute.

Americans know they are obsessed with their health (particularly jogging and new diets) and their minds ('What's on your mind, if you will allow the overstatement?') and they are terribly concerned about racial problems or 'the ethnics', by which they mean everyone who isn't immediately recognizable as typically American (a breed which by definition doesn't exist except in as much as such a stereotype is so perceived by foreigners). To quote Lewis Mumford, 'their national flower is the concrete cloverleaf', and they have strange attitudes to taxation, sex and religion – typified by the New York cleric who was allowed by the Internal Revenue to claim his subscription to *Playboy* against his tax return, but not *The Wall Street Journal* since the latter 'lacked social relevance'.

BRITISH PERCEPTIONS OF THEMSELVES

The British in turn believe that they have masses of sang-froid (as they have such strong views about the French, let us call it stiff-upper-lipism). They will not – as befits an island race, inhabitants of a jewel set in a silver sea – be bullied, tolerate injustice or cruelty to animals or accept that their policemen (bobbies) should be armed. They believe in the Queen and the rule of law. They have fought off the Vikings, Napoleon, the Kaiser, Hitler, General Galtieri and the EEC single handed. They are prepared, equally, to fight off what they believe is an American-originated invasion of everything from hippies through herpes to AIDS. They invented parliamentary democracy, tennis and golf and, consequently, they believe that God (though not the Bishop of Durham) is almost certainly an Englishman – English, not one of the other three British nations, since each of the others has outstandingly ungodly characteristics.

Fact and fiction conveniently merge over the chosen British topics of conversation, which universally relate to the weather, cricket (England only), rugby (especially Wales), soccer (everywhere), golf (especially Scotland, where it was born), snooker and darts (especially north of a highly significant town called Watford – a geographical curiosity discussed later). They are modestly proud (though Americans will claim that they have plenty to be modest about) of their culinary abilities, even though admitting that American influences have some saving graces in this field. Thus a recent visitor to a Glasgow hotel restaurant summoned the waiter to complain that the wine he had ordered was corked. 'Och, aye,' said the waiter, 'since that American chain bought up our hotel the wine bottles are all corked. We've got rid of all that metal screw-topped stuff.'

THE REALITY

BRITAIN

A country of bad weather, cricket and one sauce.

ANON

Unless, of course, you still wish to hold to your beginner-style prejudices, let us move on to the reality. The truth will, mark you, be just as odd and unexpected.

We've taken a quick, flip look at what the British aren't and what they think they themselves are; but what is the real truth? An essential here is to look at the four current tribal groupings that make up the United Kingdom. Pedants may argue that we are about to be less than historically accurate. They will bore you about the original tribes: Angles, Saxons, Normans, Picts, Celts, Scots and all that forcibly in-jected Viking blood that came along with the rape and pillage ten centuries ago, to name but a few. Forget them. The fol-lowing is what matters: the Scots (never Scotch, which is whisky – with no 'e', remember), English, Welsh and (North-ern) Irish. Let us, with prejudice, glance at them in turn.

First a proverbial encapsulation of character:

> The Scots keep the Sabbath and all else that they can get their hands on.

> The Welsh pray on their knees on Sundays and on their neighbours the rest of the week.

> The Irish know not what they believe in, but will fight anyone for it.

> The English consider themselves self-made men, thereby relieving the Almighty of a terrible responsibility.

THE WELSH

Here is a theme that never fails
To write or talk upon.
The Undersigned has been in Wales
Jonah was but in One.
THOMAS HOOD, 1836

They sing a great deal (often well), particularly in male voice choirs. They are nationalistic and a sizeable proportion of them (19 per cent) speak Welsh. They keep a fire of welcome burning – usually some Englishman's holiday cottage. They are a hardy race, stocky and small in keeping with their strong mining tradition, and they breed a good race of poets (well there's Dylan Thomas, at least) and rugby players. The lilt in the Welsh voice is excellently beguiling for storytelling, sermon delivery (particularly Methodist) and speechmaking. Their detractors call them devious and mean. In the popular view North Wales is mountains, South Wales is deep industrial valleys, black with coal dust. Neither is either. There is something about them that reminds one a bit of the Frank Crow rhyme:

Roses are red, violets are blue,
I'm a schizophrenic and so am I.

The novelist Gwyn Thomas summarized his homeland thus: 'There are still parts of Wales where the only concession to gaiety is a striped shroud.' Dylan Thomas (no relation – as far as we know) was even more succinct: 'Land of my fathers! They can bloody well keep it!' Another view by Thomas of the underlying value of his native land was demonstrated by the name of *Under Milk Wood*'s town, Llaregub (the original spelling until the BBC objected) which is, approximately, 'Bugger all' spelt backwards.

THE SCOTS

It is never difficult to distinguish between a Scotsman
with a grievance and a ray of sunshine.

P. G. WODEHOUSE

Resilient, parsimonious, alcoholic, religious, bathed (to a
greater or lesser degree) in the history of Caledonia, coming
from 'a land of Calvin and oatcakes', to quote Sidney Smith,
the Scots are particularly noticeable outside Scotland. They
turn up in large numbers (some English-educated by way of
disguise) in the top echelons of commerce, industry, politics,
the professions and the Civil Service. As Samuel Johnson said,
'It is not so much to be lamented that Old England is lost as
that the Scotch have found it,' while he argued that '... the
noblest prospect which a Scotchman ever sees is the high
road, that leads him to England.' (Johnson was bad on the
spelling rule.) The most hard-nosed capitalists and the most
intransigent union leaders often face each other on television
screens, arguing with voices that carry almost identical accents. It is a country that has long exported its talent, and
not just south of the border. Thus: John Paul Jones, Andrew
Carnegie, Alexander Graham Bell and the men who built San
Francisco's cablecar system and the first golf course in the
United States of America. Yes, they invented golf, whisky and
the steam engine. Yes, they're still at it, thereby attracting
the jealousy of their southern inferiors (as Michael Shea, who
is Scottish, puts it) such as Charles Lamb, who confessed, 'I
have been trying all my life to like Scotchmen, and am obliged
to desist from the experiment in despair.' (Lamb was no better
than Johnson at spelling.)

That's one thing about the Scots that the English are unanimous about. James Barrie said in 1908, 'There are few
more impressive sights in the world than a Scotsman on the
make.' And the Earl of Birkenhead confirmed it in 1928:
'Scotland is renowned as the home of the most ambitious
race in the world.' George Bernard Shaw was positively gen-

erous about their brain power: 'God help England if she had
no Scots to think for her!' An anonymous saying declares: 'If
you see a man wearing a kilt in England, you think he's a
Scot. If you see a man wearing a kilt in Scotland, you think
he's a Highlander. If you see a man wearing a kilt in the
Highlands, you know he's an American.' Few real Scots wear
kilts or eat porridge outside Scotland. Wherever they are
though, they tend to take their whisky neat.

THE (NORTHERN) IRISH

Northern Ireland has a problem for every solution.

TRAD.

The English should give Ireland Home Rule – and reserve
the motion picture rights.

WILL ROGERS

Now here, definitions become very important. Northern Ireland, otherwise known as the Six Counties or sometimes as
Ulster, is an integral part of the United Kingdom. Despite the
press it has had over the years – there is a story that when
a passenger plane is approaching Aldergrove Airport, Belfast,
the pilot tells the passengers to put their watches back three
hundred years to local time, 1690 – Northern Ireland is in
the main a very happy and peaceful place to live. Its rural
scenery is superb and transatlantic visitors will find it a lot
safer too (as the statistics of homicides, rapes, muggings,
armed robberies, etc., prove) than living in dear old Chicago,
NYC or LA, though, as the old saying has it, the Irish (all
varieties) still tend to ignore anything they cannot fight or
drink.

Thus, for the gentle tourist, perhaps the best advice is to
treat the Irish question with wise caution; listen rather than
utter; sup from the bowl of conventional wisdom on the subject with the length of spoon that you would use when sup-
ping with the Devil. And just remember, they claim that no

less than fifteen Presidents of the United States have a so-
called Scots–Irish (or Ulster) ancestry: John Adams, John
Quincy Adams, Monroe, Jackson, Polk, Buchanan, Johnson,
Grant, Arthur, Cleveland, Harrison, McKinley, Theodore
Roosevelt, Woodrow Wilson and JFK (not to mention Ronald
Reagan's more recent revelations of his Irish ancestry),
which, as they say, must prove something. (We are still work-
ing on what it is.)

Sellar and Yeatman had the final word about it in their
book *1066 and All That*: 'He [Gladstone] spent his declining
years trying to guess the answer to the Irish question. Unfortunately whenever he was getting warm, the Irish secretly
changed the question.'

THE ENGLISH*

Ah yes, the English. The English are compulsive pessimists,
bemoaners of their lot. They are insular and undemonstrative
(except on great national occasions) in that they do not flaunt
their emotions (like kissing) in public. It wouldn't do. Not
quite nice, etc.; though in certain metropolitan circles, the
Gallic greeting of kissing on both cheeks (known as double-
decker bussing) is a growing phenomenon. Even terribly ex-
citing sporting moments will (supporters of certain soccer
teams apart) produce lower decibel-scale cheers than on com-
parable grandstands anywhere else in the world.

The English eat roast beef and Yorkshire pudding (a stodgy,
baked batter), fish (in stodgy batter) and chips, drink warm
beer, take tea (Indian or China), watch cricket incessantly
and complain that if it's not raining, it's about to. Every time
the sun comes out and the temperature rises above the low
norm, the English go as mad as their tabloid newspaper headlines on the lines of 'England bakes', 'Phew. What a scorcher',
and so on. While an American's first question will be 'What

* By Michael Shea; the English David Frost remains discreetly silent.

do you do?', the Englishman asks 'Where do you live?', since that, like accepted or regional accents, will immediately grade and classify the respondent.

Unlike Americans who talk when they have nothing to say, the English, even when they have something to say, are still content to say nothing. England is also the land of some of the greatest eccentrics – and bores – to be found anywhere. But when Armageddon arrives, the English will be there with (depending on class) their chipped mugs of tea and their bangers or, their champagne as cool as their crustless cucumber sandwiches, talking rainfall statistics. As Shaw said, 'You will never find an Englishman in the wrong. He does everything on principle. He fights you on patriotic principles; he robs you on business principles; he enslaves you on imperial principles.' How, therefore, can what an Englishman believes be heresy? It is a contradiction in terms.

THE WATFORD GAP

Now please promptly forget what we've just said about the UK being four nations. In fact, it's five. The Scots, the Irish (Northern), the Welsh and the English who live south of Watford and the English who live north of Watford. Watford is a small and otherwise insignificant town a few miles north of London (recently enhanced by the fact that Mr Elton John the pop singer, bought and transformed their local soccer club). As is well known, English people who live north of Watford are socially deprived, survive on chip butties (a sandwich filled with French fries, we think), have outside earth closets – one to a street – and race greyhounds or pigeons. Beyond this point, Londoners and the blasé inhabitants of the South-East of England know nowhere, until they hit Scotland. Most can then identify Glasgow on the left, Edinburgh on the right and the Highlands beyond. American visitors to the UK, sightseeing in London, Windsor, Oxford, Cambridge and Stratford-upon-Avon, before moving on to Scotland, Wales or

Ireland, in search of golf, their ancestors or cheaper hotels, probably will only ever meet the south-of-Watford Englishman.

All in all, the British are very parochial. One Chairman of the English Tourist Board admitted that most overseas visitors don't know what, let alone where, Birmingham is. Quite right. Although it is England's second largest city, with a population of more than a million, most people in the UK don't know where Birmingham is either. So it is hardly surprising that when it comes to new immigrants, while Britain has a longer history than the United States does of harbouring the oppressed, they don't have an equivalent of the Statue of Liberty (though they do have, somewhat bewilderingly, a statue of Eros at Piccadilly Circus). This is because the average Brit hopes that any 'huddled masses yearning to breathe free' are only passing through on their way to somewhere else. Of the ones who have stayed, they reluctantly tolerate Irish immigrants as labourers, Asians as shopkeepers and West Indians to keep British transport running unless it's on strike. But the word is 'tolerate', *not* 'accept'. The only Asians and West Indians they truly accept are cricketers', the only Irishmen, broadcasters.

THE FAMOUS BRITISH RESERVE

The truth, held to be self-evident, is that the Brits (a flip, neo-patriotic term which originated in the USA, but they now use for themselves, particularly when comparing themselves with foreigners) are much more reserved than Americans. They even laugh (moderately, of course) at the story of one famous guidebook which mischievously encouraged foreign visitors always to introduce themselves effusively and intimately to neighbours and strangers when travelling on British public transport. So what's funny about that, you may ask. If you don't know, here's a piece of immediate advice: don't. Equally, it's just about all right to have ambition; it's all wrong to show it. Some British schools (public or private) try to instil it in their fledglings. It's called effortless superiority. But it often comes out as just being a good loser – a very popular trait in Britain. The country's leading snooker player, Mr Steve Davis, for example, only became beloved in his native land when he *lost* his world championship. And if Mr John McEnroe can only manage to lose at Wimbledon a couple more times, even he will become beloved in the British Isles too.

AMERICA

America! half brother of the world!
With something good and bad of every land.
PHILIP JAMES BAILEY

He is quite right. Something good and something bad there is. As Al Capone said, 'I never knocked the American system.' But when did he have to?

No matter where the British traveller first sets foot in God's crucible, the United States, he or she will be immediately informed that wherever that is, it is simply not like the *real* America. This is particularly true of arrivals in New York, Washington, the South, the Deep South, the West Coast or New England. Presumably what is left is so-called middle America, but ask the others whether even *that* is the real America. Americans particularly like being rude about other parts of their own country, thus from a New Yorker, 'The difference between yoghourt and L.A. is that the former has a living culture', or to quote Harry Ruby, 'Living in California adds ten years to a man's life and those extra ten years I'd like to spend in New York.' What is demonstrated by this lack of unity of view (or amazing degree of unity), is that just as none of the various parts of the United States are typical, neither are the peoples that inhabit them.

Yet in the amalgam the Americans are indeed unique, uni-

versal, united, unisonant. They have a commonality that out-
weighs their individuality. Group them as one and they rebel.
Try to split them, categorize or pigeonhole them and they
cement together, united under the Stars and Stripes, particularly in their love of deriding their own institutions, e.g.,
Will Rogers: 'I don't make jokes. I just watch the government
and report the facts.' They are, to misquote John Bright on
Disraeli, 'a nation of self-made men, who worship their crea-
tors'.

Visitors often make the mistake of trying to establish a
pattern. Forget it. The divisions, moral, cultural and social,
happened more or less by accident. It's all incongruous, all
inexplicable. How else would you get sin-packed Nevada sharing a long border with the most straight-laced of all the states,
Utah? To ask a Salt Lake City elder what he thinks of his
neighbours is rather like asking a lamp post what it thinks
about dogs. Or how else do you explain the difference between
go-getting Massachusetts and the peace and calm a mere hop
away in verdant Vermont and gentle New Hampshire? Why
does San Diego, the tenth largest city in America, almost on
the border with Mexico and a Navy town to boot, have so
much lower a crime rate than Los Angeles? And, incidentally,
nobody has yet come up with a reasonable explanation as to
why Southern California is so different from the North. (No:
the weather won't do.) In short, it's a sociologist's nightmare,
or paradise.

It's all very confusing. Sinclair Lewis said, 'Intellectually I
know that America is no better than any other country;
emotionally I know that she is better than any other country.'
And G. K. Chesterton expressed the paradox thus: 'There is
nothing the matter with Americans except their ideals: the
real American's all right; it is the ideal American who is all
wrong.'

There's only one solution. . . .

THINK REGIONAL

First and foremost, you've got to realize that the United States is a varied country because its climate, geography and peoples are so varied. It's a very cold country, a very warm country, except for where it's warm/cold all the year round. It's a rich country, able to grow anything, with enormous raw and natural resources. Not only does it have everything, it also has the communications, roads, rail, sea, air to get what it has to where it wants the stuff to go. When it doesn't have what it wants or has it and can't use it, America is second to none in terms of adapting. If there's one keyword in American history it is that: adaptability. They also like to make you feel comfortable and at home. Thus, 'Well, did you do any fornicating this weekend?' as Richard Nixon said to David Frost in an attempt at small talk at the time of the 1977 television interviews.

Remember the observation by Oliver Wendell Holmes, 'Good Americans when they die go to Paris.' Oh, really? Not quite sure about that. But of course Holmes was born in 1809 and didn't realize the effect of two World Wars, Charles de Gaulle and the *défi Americain* business. Now good Americans when they die would never be seen dead in Paris. They stay foursquare and six foot deep in the US of A. But in which part?

WASHINGTON

Washington is the only place where sound travels faster than light.

C. V. R. THOMPSON

Despised and rejected by any right-thinking American, it is nonetheless the seat of the fount of honour, the political pinnacle, the home of the President, the Pentagon, Potomac fever, careerism, the State Department and Georgetown hostesses. Bitterly cold in winter, unbearably hot and humid in summer, its variegated weather is as wide-ranging as the political and social opinions of the city's native inhabitants or are represented by those who temporarily reside there. Washington *is* – although sometimes it appears like an empty shell. Despite the mega-rat-race to get there, you won't find many Americans who actually like the place.

In the words attributed to JFK, 'a city of Southern efficiency and Northern charm'.

NEW ENGLAND

New England is famous for its intellectual élitism and its weather. To quote Eric Knighton on the first and Joseph Wood Krutch on the second,

> You can always tell the Irish,
> You can always tell the Dutch,
> You can always tell a Yankee,
> But you cannot tell him much.
> *All Yankees are Liars*

The most serious charge which can be brought against New England is not Puritanism but February.
> *The Twelve Seasons*

THE SOUTH

In the South, the Civil War is what AD is elsewhere: they date from it.

ANON.

Greatly misunderstood, and though the Civil War is well over a century past, the scars still show. Henry Miller said: 'The Old South was ploughed under, but the ashes are still warm.' There is still a lot of mystique about, alongside tough atti-

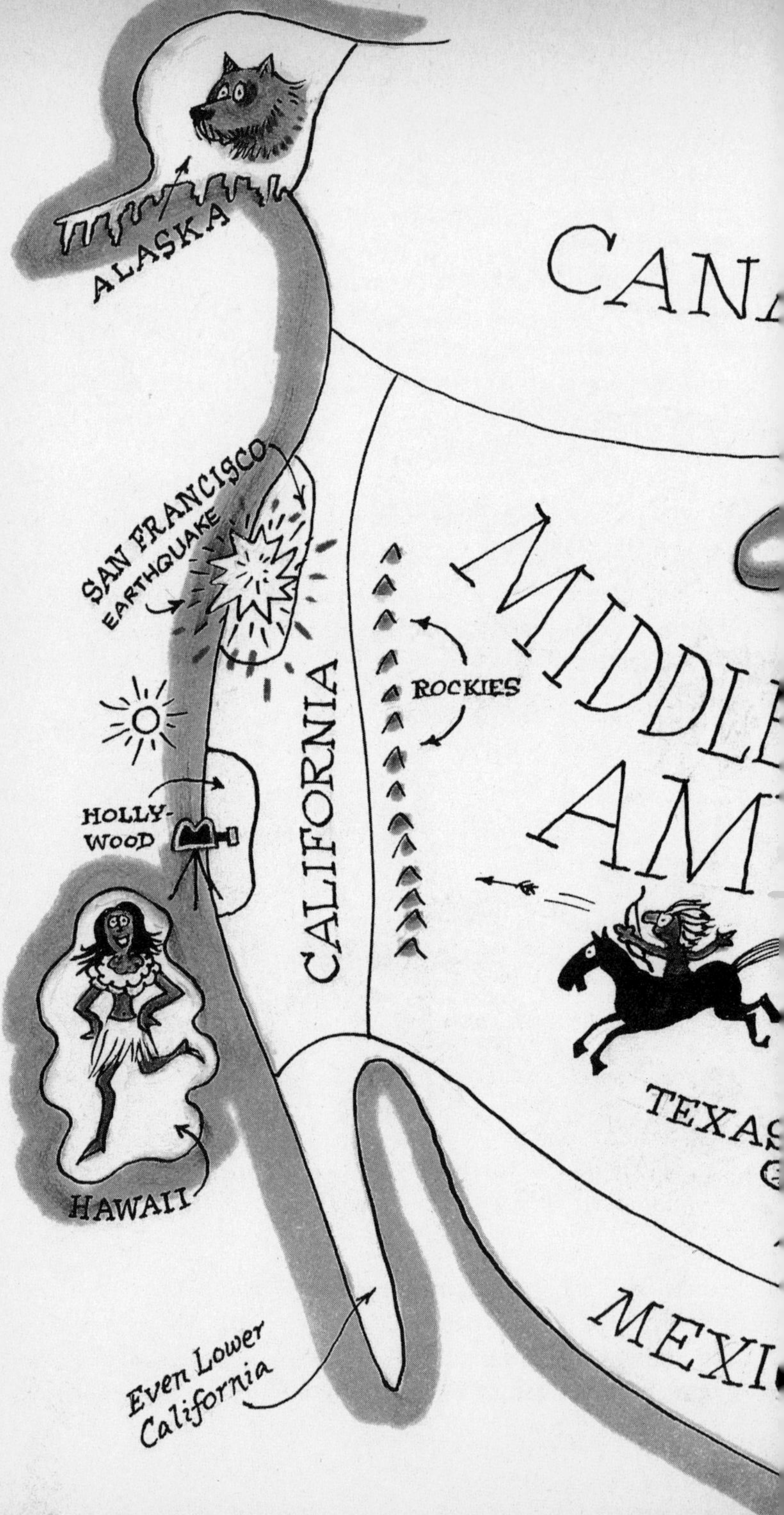

ALASKA

CANA[DA]

SAN FRANCISCO
EARTHQUAKE

ROCKIES

MIDDLE
AM[ERICA]

CALIFORNIA

HOLLY-
WOOD

HAWAII

TEXAS

MEXI[CO]

Even Lower
California

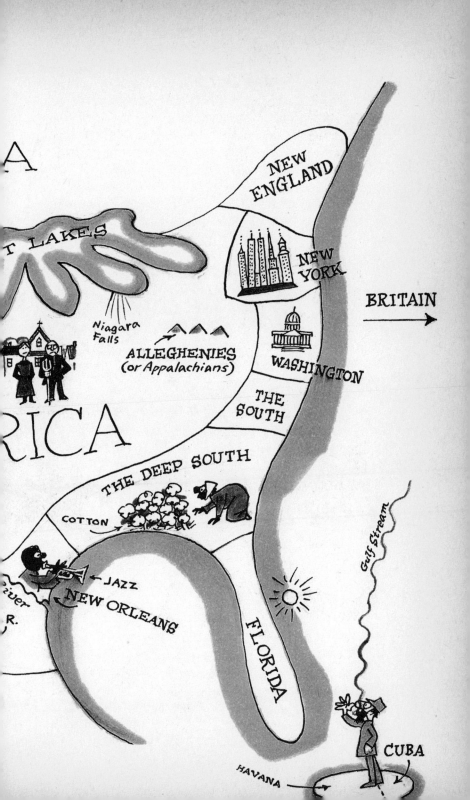

tudes, both political and social. But it's also all out for growth, as soap opera fans the world over will easily recognize. Even more important, it is now a founder member of the Sunbelt, which is rapidly taking over the country. The South also incorporates country music, and its capital, Nashville, which tries to seem a respectable city of business and Southern gentility, but at its heart is pure showbiz: everyone who lives there is, has been, or knows someone who is, cutting a record. Then there is the *Deep South*, which is all of the above only more so.

THE MIDWEST

The Midwest, or Middle America, runs for at least a thousand miles, from Pittsburgh to the Rockies, and is everything that isn't the other bits, plus Chicago. Its flat landscape remains much the same all the way. To say that it's boring is, to some, heaping it with far too much praise. In 1944 Freya Stark wrote, 'If California had been in the middle, and the Middle West on this far side, I don't believe anyone would have bothered to come so far.' But it is *the* realest of real America.

In the words of Arthur Chapman in 1916:

> Out where the handclasp's a little stronger,
> Out where the smile dwells a little longer,
> That's where the West begins.

It's full of cowpokes, and is not known for its night life.

FLORIDA

This finger pointing downward towards the Caribbean is held by some to be a colony of Cuba, by others, a paradise of senior citizens' colonies ('eventide homes'), and people who believe in 'life, liberty and the happiness of pursuit'. It is said that it was a Florida hospital patient who, when approached by a young intern wielding a hypodermic and explaining, 'Just a little prick with a needle', said, 'I know you are, but what are you going to do with the needle?'

GRAND CANYON

A hole in the ground in Arizona, though of frankly Texan proportions, conveniently situated for the moment when Americans finally decide to get rid of Las Vegas.

LAS VEGAS

Sin City, with facilities for every sort of gambling, from slot machines to instant marriage and extra-marital sex, which 'between a man and a woman', as someone said 'can be wonderful – provided you get between the right man and the right woman'.

PALM SPRINGS

A desert haven for rich Californians. Scientists have discovered that the summer temperature is, within two degrees, exactly as cool as the residents' disdain for outsiders.

ABSOLUTELY ALL YOU NEED TO KNOW ABOUT LOS ANGELES

I attended a dinner the other morning given for the Old Settlers of California. No one was allowed to attend unless he had been in the State two and a half years.

WILL ROGERS

Los Angeles is half as big as Luxembourg, but with about fourteen times as many inhabitants and roughly seventy-three times as many radio stations.

The sprawling mega-metropolis of the Western world, it is a city of swimming pools, salads, soap operas and satellite dishes. Nestled among the car parks, the nature-lover can still find refreshing pockets of greenery – nowadays called Astro-turf. As the place has got bigger, its name has got shorter. Back in 1781 it was called El Pueblo de Nuestra Señora de Los Angeles de Porciuncula – a name so brutally abbreviated over the centuries that all that now remains are the last two letters.

Woody Allen's famous line that Los Angeles' only cultural advantage is being able to turn right on a red light still rings true. It is a city of light and cars, smog and glare, where the men are strong and the women are reconditioned. Tremendous attention is paid to bodies (human) and automobiles. People are much less formal than in New York, in the way they dress (barely covering many parts or wearing jumpsuits) and the way they talk. Most talk is about cars or driving. For example, if you are hapless enough to have forgotten to turn on your car headlights, you'll hear a chorus of 'LIGHTS, ASSHOLE!' A few years ago, before people started pumping their own gas and when the smog wasn't quite as thick, they would have merely said, 'LIGHTS!' (Incidentally, which British visitor was it who said, when telephoning from a call-box: 'I'm calling from a phone box at the corner of Walk and Don't Walk.'?)

Much of the language comes out of EST, Werner Erhard's training, or surfer talk. Valley Girl talk comes out of spending days at shopping malls (some are totally awesome). If you don't look 'like really cute', then you're 'totally bagged out'. When at a mall, you 'cruise' looking for a 'totally cool dude'. If he's 'like a totally major, maximum cool dude', he's 'vicious'. Other California lingo comes from mispronouncing Spanish words; and in LA, it is only fitting that restaurant row would be on a swamp (that's what La Cienega means).

Contained within the 'City of Angels' is 'Tinseltown', otherwise Hollywood – a purveyor of glamour, glitter and, yes, garbage to the world. Indeed Marina del Rey, a very expensive resort marina, is actually built on the site of the old city rubbish dump. 'California', as Fred Allen said, 'is a great place – if you happen to be an orange.' It's also the only place in the world where you can rent a limousine with a built-in jacuzzi – or would feel the need to. Disneyland can also be found in Los Angeles. Wherever you look.

THE FIFTY STATES

The fifty states are an unending source of confusion. First the visitor must rid himself of the apparently logical idea that the capital of the state will be the most important city in the state. Not a bit of it. There may be one or two states with a logical choice (Atlanta for Georgia, Boston for Massachusetts and Indianapolis – almost compulsorily – for Indiana), but in general the combination of historical tact and diplomacy, jealousy and plain sloppy thinking has left Tallahassee rather than Miami as the capital of Florida, Springfield rather than Chicago as the capital of Illinois, Jefferson City rather than St Louis as the capital of Missouri and Baton Rouge rather than New Orleans as the capital of Louisiana.

As if that was not confusing enough, next there are the nicknames. After a few deceptively easy examples – Alabama is the Cotton State and Hawaii is the Aloha State (rather than, say, Alaska) – questions come thick and fast. Why is Iowa the Hawkeye State, but Ohio the Buckeye State? And how do the various states establish their prior claims to assorted animals? Minnesota is the Gopher State, Oregon gets the beaver, South Dakota is the Coyote State and Wisconsin proudly proclaims itself the Badger State. (No state has as yet claimed the ferret.)

For reasons that are beyond us, Utah manages to claim to be the Beehive State, and New Jersey prides itself – with a certain lack of credibility – on being the Garden State, but there are deeper mysteries to come: what made Missouri call itself the Show Me State and why, of all the states you could choose, should Arkansas – yes, Arkansas – have won the title The Wonder State?

The state songs are not wildly inventive. Alabama hit on a song called *Alabama*, Arizona hit on a song called *Arizona*, Rhode Island hit on a song called *Rhode Island* and really only Oklahoma has any excuse. There's *Michigan, My Michigan*, *Oregon, My Oregon* and just for a change of pace *Texas, Our Texas*. Not to mention the award-winningly lame *Here We Have Idaho*.

When it comes to state mottoes, there are the worthy ones which opt for 'Liberty and Independence' (Delaware); 'Virtue, Liberty and Independence' (Pennsylvania); and 'Freedom and Unity' (Vermont). Tennessee is somewhat more practical – it opts for 'Agriculture and Commerce'; and Montana is down-right brazen – none of this liberty and virtue stuff for them – just simple straightforward 'Gold and Silver'.

There are some interesting contrasts. Ohio claims, 'With God All Things Are Possible', but Oklahoma declares, 'Labor Conquers All Things'. Then there are the slightly more be-wildering mottoes. Connecticut says, 'He Who Transplanted Still Sustains', possibly a reference to an early heart surgeon. West Virginia claims, 'Mountaineers Are Always Free'. Clim-ber friends of the authors say, 'Nonsense – they can be very expensive.' Maryland, in what is conceivably an early tribute to Margaret Thatcher, opts for 'Manly Deeds, Womanly Words' and Virginia proudly proclaims the motto 'Thus Al-ways To Tyrants' without explaining where thus is. Though even that is not as problematical as the answer to the ques-tion: 'What is *it*?' California's motto is 'I Have Found *It*', while Idaho says, '*It* Is Forever' but on the other hand New Mexico says, '*It* Grows As *It* Goes'. *It* is all very confusing. (Michigan, incidentally, wins the 'Here We Have Idaho' award with the motto 'If you seek a pleasant peninsula look around you'.)

The above should at least give the unwary (or even wary)

traveller in the US something to start a conversation with in most of the fifty states. If there is still an awkward pause, we recommend you add a few of the bizarre facts that the States proclaim about themselves. These can be used either as statements or as the basis of a latter-day version of Trivial Pursuits. Did you know, for example, that the state bird of New Mexico is the roadrunner and that of Delaware is the blue

hen chicken? Did you know that dogwood is both the state flower and the state tree of Virginia? Did you know that West Virginians observe the 55 mph speed limit more scrupulously than the drivers of any other state or that Wichita, Kansas, boasts the highest percentage of church attendance in the United States? It may even have escaped your notice that fewer sightings of Unidentified Flying Objects have been reported in Massachusetts than any other state in the Union; or that less than 1.3% of Michigan residents spend their holidays in Africa.

By now your cocktail party will be agog – and you can drive home the advantage. Did your awed listeners know that the consumption of Adriatic figs in St Louis has risen by 87% in the last two years? Or that Omaha, Nebraska, consumes more tomato juice per head of the population than anywhere else in the nation? (All this despite the fact that the use of laxatives in Cleveland, Ohio, has declined by 17% since 1981.) And there's more – much more! State dental officials in Georgia estimate that approximately 2,500 pairs of false

teeth lie at the bottom of the Flint River. The Franksville Specialty Company of Conover, Wisconsin, manufactures

brassieres for cows up to size 108. And fewer than 1% of all telephone calls placed in Wyoming are to South Korea (though state officials, you will be happy to hear, expect this to change as the next Olympics approach).

By now your devoted audience will be convinced that you have read more state guide books than all of them put together, so apply the *coup de grace*: a city ordinance passed in Charleston, South Carolina, in 1975 required horse owners to put nappies on their horses. Selling cotton at night in Mississippi can result in a fine of $500. In Gary, Indiana, it is illegal to go to the theatre within four hours of eating garlic (which is probably why one of the authors, at least, tries to

confine his theatre-going to Gary, Indiana). And, above all, you cannot legally lasso a fish in Knoxville, Tennessee. So there.

2
A Tale of Two Cities

"

In New York the earth seems to spin more quickly round its axis.

HERBERT BEERBOHM TREE

A city where everyone mutinies but no one deserts.

HARRY HERSHFIELD

This rocky island, this concrete Capri.

CYRIL CONNOLLY

London! It has the sound of distant thunder.

JAMES BONE

London is a university with ten million graduates qualified to live and let live.

OLIVER ST JOHN GOGARTY

"

NEW YORK

Even if you are someone lucky enough to spend a lot of his time in London, New York is still quite simply special. From the moment you arrive. The airports are named after politicians, of all people. (Mrs Thatcher will have made a note of that.) The cars are three feet longer, the limousines three yards longer, than the last ones you saw seven and a half hours ago – a thoughtful touch given the condition of the roads that the visitor is about to encounter. If your flight is the last of the day, arriving at 9.30, your arrival at the hotel at 10.30 pm (3.30 am London time) will be followed by the first of several somewhat disorientating (though oddly sincere) instructions to 'Have a nice day.' (After a glorious shower of unaccustomed hurricane-like intensity and supper, the greeting to the weary traveller returning to the hotel at 1.00 am will of course have been somewhat updated to 'Have a nice evening.'

Then there is Broadway. You will find it has an excitement that the West End lacks. The actor starring on Broadway who arrives late at a dinner party is saluted, and the hostess immediately makes a place for him on her right. The actor starring in the West End who arrives late is apologetic, and the hostess consigns him to wait in the room where coffee is going to be served, while the diners continue with their dessert.

Later still in the evening, as clubs like Studio 54 fade from the memory, other clubs spring up. Some basic rules apply. In general it helps to get in if you arrive by limo. Most clubs these days approve of wealth, so look rich. For men: polyester is out, as are pot bellies, gold neck chains, glasses with initials in the lens bottoms, and hairpieces. For women: don't attempt a Cyndi Lauper look unless you have enormous personal style; Farrah-type hair is out, as are synthetic animal prints if you are overweight.

New York Magazine recently announced that eating in restaurants has replaced theatre, movies and sex as pastimes for busy New Yorkers. That's because most people work hard and have little time to buy or prepare food, and have tiny kitchens. Chinatown and Little Italy are great for inexpensive, interesting Chinese and Italian meals, respectively; there's a strip on Seventh Street, off Second Avenue, that has about fourteen Indian restaurants. The only problem with that Seventh Street strip is that you get the feeling that the person serving you used to be a nuclear physicist in his native country and that he is not amused by his new job.

A word about New York delicatessens: There are still several authentic New York delis, i.e., places that serve enormous bowls of beef barley or chicken matzo ball soup and sandwiches that are as thick as the New York phone book. When taking a bite of these sandwiches, your chin goes into your chest and your nose into your scalp. Favourites are corned beef on rye, pastrami, tongue, turkey, or combinations of all four. (Don't ever put mayonnaise on a meat sandwich.) A good deli has a bowl of pickles and sour tomatoes sitting on the table at all times; you eat them until you feel stuffed. Then you order. It's *de rigueur.* And if your waiter is nice to you, something is very wrong. Tell him again that you're from out of town.

New York means many different things to different people. To the authors it certainly means cheesecake, more species of cheesecake than they ever knew existed: rum, orange, hazelnut, chocolate marble, Italian, Boston and, of course, New York. It means the chestnut vendors on Fifth Avenue. Some people find New Yorkers rude; on the contrary, we find the shop assistants almost uniformly warm and welcoming. David Frost well remembers on his first visit to New York the sense of shock that he felt when having said, 'Thank you,' the shop assistant replied, 'You're welcome.' He was astonished. 'Thank you,' he said with renewed gratitude. 'You're welcome,' she said again. 'Thank you,' he said again. If he had not been late for the airport, he might still be there now.

At the same time, many people in service industries do develop contrary natures; their immediate response to any simple request is negative. This requires a bit of patience and perseverance on your part. If you enter a dry cleaner that advertises 'one-hour Martinizing' for example, and ask for same-day service for a suit, expect some flak. One typical response: 'You're pressuring me; I don't need that kind of pressure.' Listen politely and then ask again for same-day service. You'll get it. (These perverse natures also result in some delightful signs, like 'The Third Best Bakery in New York'.)

The current New York motto would seem to be, 'This is ridiculous!' This phrase is the release valve that every New Yorker needs. It comes in handy in a city where one must wait hours in the cold to get into a movie theatre, or pay $1,500 a month for a studio apartment, or put up with a

jackhammer outside one's bedroom window for months;
while enduring these hardships, it makes most New Yorkers
feel better to repeat the phrase, over and over, like a mantra.

Now that casual sex is out, most Manhattanspeak centres
on food, real estate, money, or exercise. One cannot overem-
phasize the importance of 'bottom line' in the language of
busy executives, the phrase issued at every conceivable turn,
even in relationship talk, 'We have to prioritize our time; the
bottom line is that I'm not sure whether I want one-on-one.'
Any apartment buying talk is highly acceptable at parties:
this includes 'balloon mortgages', 'closing' (that's when the
co-op or condo you've tried to buy is finally yours), 'flipping'
your apartment – if the apartment you live in has 'gone
condo (or co-op)' you get an 'insider's price' and can either
buy it or 'flip it'. Also body-building talk is all the rage; you
'bulk up' (that means you're going for muscle instead of definition) and eat your 'carbo load' (runners especially are big
on whole-wheat pasta). 'Feel the burn' is a phrase popularized
by Jane Fonda. Since New Yorkers are eating out instead of
having sexual relations (see above), the new aphrodisiac
seems to be an American Express Card flashed by the woman
in inviting a man out to dinner. Once there, he can whisper
words like *arrugula* or *radicchio* in her ear.

A bit of correct mumbo-jumbo will also not go amiss during
your visit. A few phrases like 'holistic psychotherapies',
'shiatsu'/'balancing your body energies', 'reflexology hotline',
'pre-op transexual' and 'bioenergetic gestalt therapy' will fill
many a pause if used on the right occasion.

The art of the one-liner is preserved for grateful generations
yet unborn on the streets of New York by the cab drivers.
David Frost well remembers a cab on a boiling July day, and
the New York traffic jam that held them stationary for twenty
minutes while they sat and sweltered. David bore it in silence
because there just seemed to be no words to express the
misery. The driver found them. 'Better maybe we never *invented* the wheel, huh?'

In terms of getting a cab, certain rules again apply. Once

you flag down a cab, never let anyone come along and claim it. Tell that person that you're giving birth or that you're about to be arrested. Unless of course it seems to be love at first sight, in which case you could suggest sharing the ride (drop him or her off; keep the cab at all costs). Tell the driver in advance if you have a $20 bill; even if it looks as though he's been driving nonstop for four days (by his beard growth and his tendency to nod off), chances are he has two single dollar bills, a dime and two pennies. Try not to talk to the driver (you'll hear about his breakdown on the Moshulu Parkway or about his ex-wife) or look at the road ahead (most manage to get you there with a mere fifty or so close calls).

There is, of course, the little matter of the New York crime rate. After all, they even had a bank robber who got mugged on the way to the getaway car. But New York muggers come in different shapes and sizes. Only recently there was an example of the gallant mugger – he stood up in a crowded subway and offered a lady his gun. But beware, above all, of the sophisticated mugger in Manhattan who has hit on a particularly devilish device: he holds up businessmen on their way home in the evening and threatens to spray them with very expensive French perfume.

Then there is the *New York Times*, unlike any other newspaper in the world in the range of its authority. Somehow one can never escape from the suspicion that, hidden among its catacombs or tucked away in its filing cabinets on Forty-Third Street, there is a Pulitzer Prize winner on almost any topic the reader could name just waiting to be called out for a brief emergence into the sunlight of the printed page. The *New York Times* covers rock music with as much care, if not quite as much enthusiasm, as it does world affairs. It steadfastly holds on to its style of calling all newmakers Mr, Miss or Mrs; in a review of bulky singer Meatloaf, they referred to him five times as 'Mr Loaf'. In Sid Vicious's obituary they explained that on stage 'Mr Vicious played the bass guitar and vomited.'

The best thing about New York is that ideas matter. Indeed it could be argued that the business of New York is to take in ideas and information from other places, reprocess them with New York know-how and sell them back at a profit. And the interchange of those ideas is aided and abetted by the very geography of the place. The island of Manhattan is a remarkably small place, 22.6 square miles, and people actually walk – which is seldom done in other parts of the States. The result is that New York is the capital of face-to-face meetings. The authors run into more friends and acquaintances in the streets of New York than anywhere else. And high on the agenda, almost immediately, are ideas – not just ideas in a vacuum, but ideas that somebody will probably be prepared to bet on.

That's why we love New York. That's why we do not mind service being 20 per cent, or even – sacrifice of sacrifices – the dearth of Cuban cigars. Or indeed even the dawning realization that in most cities people do not feel the need to say, 'Have a nice day,' because it never occurs to them to fear that it may be a nasty one.

Dr Johnson said, 'A man who is tired of London is tired of life', and he was probably right. But a man who is tired of New York is tired of thought. And work. And cheesecake.

LONDON

Before you even land in London you will notice the greenery: the parks and commons, the garden squares, and everywhere the carefully tended gardens of private houses, large and small. England is not so much a nation of shopkeepers – or even shoplifters – as a nation of gardeners. Indeed you will find that normally sane people whom you would expect to breathe a sigh of relief at finding a house with no large garden to look after go out and rent themselves an allotment so they can drive down the road and voluntarily commit themselves to the hard work and drudgery they have just been saved from at home.

But we are only just landing at Heathrow, and immediately there is more good news. The journey from Heathrow airport (*not* named after a recent Tory Prime Minister, incidentally) into the centre of London is a remarkably easy one. You may not find the driver of the upright, comfortable black cab quite as loquacious as his New York counterpart, but you will find him a great deal better informed about his city. And there is no danger at all that he will tell you proudly that he is a new immigrant and then ask you for directions.

If you find the number of television and radio channels a little less than a horn of plenty, there is compensation coming in the morning. Not just one newspaper as in some American cities, or two as in Los Angeles or three as in New York, but nine – count them – nine. With every variation the heart could desire: from the equivalent of the *National Enquirer* (called the *Sun*) to that of the *Wall Street Journal* (called the

Financial Times). Since it is now being printed simultaneously in the States, American business readers will understand the local joke: 'What's always pink and hard and comes every morning?' Answer: 'The *Financial Times* crossword.'

Londoners can be very thoughtful and unselfish. After all, they have even kept lowering the value of their pound to try and meet the value of your dollar. You will find that the London policeman accepts that part of his job is acting as a tourist guide. (This is not always the case, as we know, with 'New York's finest'.) You will discover a plenitude of double-decker buses, and on the older ones with platforms you can even climb on when they are moving or when they have stopped at traffic lights. And the seats on the subway are *upholstered*!

Londoners do not promote themselves very well. It is as difficult to imagine an 'I Love New York' type campaign taking off in London as it is to imagine Britishers singing their national anthem with the zeal that Americans launch into theirs. Maybe it's all to do with the shyness and understatement of Londoners versus the openness and even brashness of New Yorkers. New Yorkers don't mind being seen in a singles bar – it's a healthy pursuit. Singles bars in London have never caught on. To a Londoner, it would be almost as bad as being caught in a dirty raincoat on the way in to a strip club. Instead of an 'I Love London' campaign, Londoners' only response over the years has been typically low-key – a series of tuneful well-written songs about such things as nightingales singing in Berkeley Square. No raucous and rousing refrains about 'London, London' sung by a local equivalent of Liza Minnelli. London pride is rarely permissible and then only because it has been 'handed down to us'.

Yet everywhere there is the past: every stage of London's history, from AD 43 when the Romans bridged the Thames until today, can be traced in London's buildings and monuments. From Westminster Abbey (where the famous men of Britain's past lie buried) and the House of Commons (where the famous men of Britain's present lie buried) to more recent relics like Carnaby Street (or Mincing Lane as it came to be known in the 1960s). Equally important to your deliberations will be Trafalgar Square, home of Nelson's Column, pigeons and stained-glass windows, and on to Cleopatra's Needle, which is 68 feet high. (Cleopatra had incredibly bad eyesight.) Then as Big Ben strikes – and negotiations begin on getting it back to work again – you can move on to the Tower of London, where Sir Walter Raleigh took his last walk around the block.

Travel as often as you can on the Thames, which contrary to rumour is a regular feature of London and not specially laid down every year for the Oxford and Cambridge Boat Race. London is a city of museums. Among the best are the Science Museum, for those interested in science; the Natural

History Museum for those interested in natural history; and the Victoria and Albert Museum, for those interested in Victoria and Albert. Ah, if only stones could talk, what a lot of boring old historical nonsense they would tell.

Don't miss London's picturesque street markets. (Ideal for anyone who wants to buy a street.) And there you will find a great local delicacy, jellied eels. These are tasteless, jelly-like cold fish in tasteless, fish-like cold jelly. Absolutely revolting, but what's tradition worth unless you suffer for it? American visitors will find that London pubs are not as old-fashioned and hidebound as they used to be. Some of the more go-ahead ones are already installing automatic beer warmers. But beware of the increasing prevalence of the game of darts, which you may find going on all about you. There is a real danger that you could get stoned and stabbed at the same time. You will find an ever-growing multitude of Italian restaurants, so it's best when you want a meal to follow the old proverb, 'When in London, do as the Romans do.'

Do not try and visit the circus in London. The only proper circus, Bertram Mills Circus, has closed. The remainder – Piccadilly, Oxford, St Giles and the rest – turn out to be merely traffic intersections. But there are compensations. Venice has its regattas, Siena its Palio, Spain her fiestas, Brazil her carnivals and Munich its beer festivals. What equivalents has London got? Well there's the famous Aldermaston March, of course, whose colourful traditions date back almost to 1956, and then there's the annual Lord Mayor's Procession. This is a festive, imaginative affair. If the Lord Mayor is in fruit exporting, there will be 200 floats taking fruit as their theme. If he's in plastic bags, the theme is plastic bags. This is why Londoners never had a fertilizer tycoon as Lord Mayor. And as if this is not entertainment enough, London has two splendid exhibition halls, Earls Court and Olympia, where you may be lucky enough to see some stirring events such as the Mechanical Handling, Ventilating Equipment and Sanitary Accessories Exhibition, often considered by quite sober men to be the best Mechanical Handling, Ventilating Equipment and Sanitary Accessories Exhibition in the world, and a must for all those who love Mechanical Handling, Ventilating Equipment and Sanitary Accessories.

Not only can you spend money elegantly in London, you can lose money more elegantly than anywhere in the United States. In the hushed confines of the Aspinall, Curzon, Clermont or several other top gaming clubs, superb food and wine and historic houses dull the pain of defeat and enhance the pleasure of victory. One danger though: the heady cocktail of class and money. If you run out of the money you can afford, for goodness' sake do not be ashamed to admit your resources are not limitless to the titled gentleman next door to you by leaving the table. He may even be quite relieved, because it will allow him to leave too.

Another word of warning: for reasons quite beyond the comprehension of the authors, one shower of rain brings traffic in London to a standstill. People have not had the time to go home and get a car because it is raining, and yet it happens. Drivers cannot be driving that much more slowly round Berkeley Square than they usually do, and yet it happens. So if it rains, double the amount of time you are going to need to get anywhere. And, as has frequently been observed, London taxis are soluble – they dissolve in the rain.

London, you will find, has two sporting cathedrals: Lord's the headquarters of cricket, and the Centre Court at Wimbledon; the only difference being that Lord's is always Lord's, but Wimbledon is only Wimbledon for two weeks a year and a suburb for the other fifty.

London is also a superb centre for touring. Even shopping in a French supermarket is just a day trip away. And New Yorkers always seem to be struck by how soon, when driving out of London, one comes to *real* countryside.

Where does all this richness and diversity come from? Partly from having been there for a long time, of course, but there is more to it than that. 'London – a nation, not a city,' wrote Disraeli back in 1870 and it's still true today. There is a completeness about London that New York, Washington and Los Angeles cannot match. Because London is all three cities in one. It is the financial and journalistic capital like New York, it is the political capital like Washington, it is the film and television capital like Los Angeles. (The only thing it is increasingly short of is capital itself.)

London is all things to all people. To the city commuter, it's merely the vast, sprawling, overcrowded city where he works, but to the tourist it's transformed into the vast sprawling, overcrowded city where he is spending his holidays. Some American tourists do London in a day. And vice versa. So take your time. Enjoy the city. And don't forget the time change. To quote Bette Midler, 'When it's three o'clock in New York, it's still 1938 in London'.

3
History Matters

"

It is interesting that more European communities have managed to survive in a pure form in America, and not in Europe.

RUTH PRAWER JHABVALA

Americans think of themselves collectively as a huge rescue operation on a twenty-four hour call to any spot on the globe where dispute and conflict may erupt.

ELDRIDGE CLEAVER

An Englishman is a man who lives on an island in the North Sea governed by Scotsmen.

PHILIP GUEDALLA

I say that if Lincoln were living today, he would turn over in his grave.

PRESIDENT GERALD FORD (*amongst others*)

History proves nothing.

ANON.

"

Remembering that history is only what you can remember, Americans realize as well as Britons that there are only three really key figures in Anglo-American relations: George III, who lost the American Colonies; Mrs Wallis Simpson, who caused Britain's greatest constitutional crisis; and Jennie Jerome, who gave the world Winston Churchill. Pedantic academics may argue that there are more. These will suffice for our purposes.

Britons visiting the States should be aware of the following key dates. If you can quote them on dazzling social occasions, you've got a full head start: history very potted indeed.

AN ESSENTIAL HISTORY OF THE UNITED STATES

1000   Leif Erikson discovers America and calls it Vinland after the well-known New England vins. (Now most of what he'd find there would be Californian.)

1492   Christopher Columbus discovers the pleasures of the Bahamas and Hispaniola, having set off to find India and thinking he'd found America instead. (We call him the Great Navigator.)

1493   Columbus finds Puerto Rico, Jamaica, etc.

1497   John Cabot (re-) discovers America.

1498   Columbus discovers Trinidad.

1502   Columbus, on his fourth voyage, finds Panama. (Ah, well. Nobody's perfect.)

1507   Martin Waldseemuller names the continent 'America'. It was called after Amerigo Vespucci, who did not lead an expedition of 1499 (the leader was one Hojeda) to Venezuela, but lied about his exploits in some letters which were turned into a book by someone else (who also forged an extra letter to improve the story). Thus the story got around that he had preceded Cabot to N. America, which in fact he never visited at all. Nor did Waldseemuller, who was a map-maker.

1524   Giovanni da Verrazano discovers the Hudson River, and finds a good place for a bridge.

1565   Billiards introduced to America from Spain.

1578   Francis Drake claims California for Britain (Britain wasn't asked).

1607   English bring civilization to Jamestown.

1609   Henry Hudson finds the river that de Verrazano has already found.

1612   John Rolfe starts curing tobacco – as a health product.

1613   Pocahontas sees the light and becomes Christian.

1618   White virgins first come to Virginia.

1619   Democracy (the House of Burgesses) comes to Virginia.

1626   Manhattan bought for $24 worth of trinkets. The first big NYC real estate deal. (Think how much those dollars would be worth today.)

1636   A Hooker founds Hartford, Connecticut.

1643   First diner opens in Boston.

1660   Massachusetts fines celebrators of Christmas 5 shillings.

1664   New Amsterdam becomes New York. Dykes banned.

1675   Long-haired men prosecuted in Massachusetts. Gays banned.

1692   Eighteen Salem witches executed. Puritanism in full swing.

1701   Brits found Yale.

1725   First New York newspaper – *The Gazette* – founded.

1751   First cricket match held in New York City. Ends in a draw after Geoff Boycott gets a parking ticket for staying at the crease too long.

1770   Cries of 'Rhubarb!' first heard in America, following its introduction by Benjamin Franklin.

1773   Boston Tea Party. Trouble brewing.

1775   Paul Revere rides to alert colonists of something ('The British are ... er ... er ...) Battle of Bunker Hill is fought on Breed's Hill (a British away win).

1776   America secedes.

1786	Ice-cream made professionally in New York City.
1789	New York becomes the capital of the United States.
1803	The US buys Louisiana from France for 3 cents an acre.
1809	First cricket club founded in Boston.
1812	Madison declares war on England. Forty-one days later, news of this reaches London.
1814	British burn down White House. Peace treaty signed at Ghent.
1815	2,000 British casualties at the Battle of New Orleans, news of the peace having yet to reach America.
1818	Amelia 'Bloomers' Bloomer wears her first diaper.
1819	US buys Florida from Spain (no price given).
1822	The US now leads the world in the making of false teeth.
1833	Baseball supersedes cricket in Philadelphia.
1840	Britain recognizes an independent Texas.
1845	Texas joins the USA.
1849	Safety-pin patented. Forty-Niners go for gold.
1851	Linus Yale locks his first doors.
1852	Queen Victoria reads *Uncle Tom's Cabin* and is much amused.
1855	King Gillette is born to shave the world.
1865	Lincoln attends a theatre performance at Ford's Theatre, Washington.

1867   US buys Alaska from Russia for 2 cents an acre.

1868   The fifteenth and only bachelor President, Buchanan, dies.

1876   Wild Bill Hickock is shot dead at poker game.

1879   Woolworths opens. Some customers still waiting to be served.

1881   President Garfield and Billy the Kid are shot dead (separately).

1882   Jesse James shot dead. Horlicks starts putting people to sleep.

1883   Brooklyn is connected to civilization by a bridge.

1886   Gustave Eiffel's Statue of Liberty dedicated. Coca Cola invented.

1890   Electric chair first used.

1892   Basketball is invented by a Canadian.

1894   Benjamin Kubelsky born. Later he turns into Jack Benny.

1896   First publicly shown 'movie' in USA. Nathan Birnbaum (otherwise George Burns) born, but does not star.

1898   US forces capture Puerto Rico and Guam.

1899   President McKinley rides in a car. Al Capone is born in Naples.

1903   First manned flight by the Wright Brothers, lasting 59 seconds. Teddy bears invented.

1906   US troops land in Cuba to quell revolt.

1907   US Marines land in Honduras to protect US lives and property. Bob Hope (aged 4) emigrates to America from Britain, by sea.

1903   Lucille Le Sueur (later Joan Crawford) and James Stewart (see 1913) born, separately.

1909   US troops help rebel forces overthrow Nicaragua's leader.

1910   Electric washing machines marketed. Father's Day invented.

1911   Ronald Reagan born.

1912   First automobile speeding offender jailed. Foxtrot invented. US Marines invade Nicaragua.

1913   James Stewart born, but this one became Stewart Grainger. Leslie Lynch King Junior born; he will grow up to become Gerald Ford.

1915   Taber runs the mile in 4 minutes 12.6 seconds. US Marines land in Haiti.

1916   US establishes naval bases in Nicaragua.

1917   US buys Virgin Islands for 25 million. Dino Crocetti, a.k.a. Dean Martin, has his first drink.

1920   Women given the vote. Prohibition follows.

1924   US Marines land in Shanghai to help suppress civil war in China. J. Edgar Hoover becomes director of the FBI. Gas chamber first used.

1926   Norma Jean Baker is born. US Marines land in Nicaragua to quell insurrection.

1927   US Marines land in Nicaragua to protect US lives and property. Lizzie Borden lays down her axe for the last time.

1928   Mickey Mouse brings fame to America.

1929   St Valentine's Day celebrations are held in Chicago.

1933   Mae West says, 'Come up and see me sometime.' Prohibition ends.

1934   John Dillinger shot dead by the FBI. US beats UK in Walker Cup.

1935   Alcoholics Anonymous set up in New York. Parking meters come to Oklahoma City.

1938   DuPont's market nylon combs and Glenn Miller forms jazz band.

1939   Nylon stockings come on the market. The Boston Red-Sox are televised for the first time.

1941   Orson Welles stars in *Citizen Kane*. Aerosol sprays are introduced.

1943   Pentagon built. Mr Biro (a Hungarian working in Argentina) first writes his name on the American wall of fame.

1945   Maureen O'Sullivan gives birth to Mia Farrow.

1946   Bikinis appear for the benefit of all mankind.

1953   *Playboy* magazine ignores the invention of the bikini.

1956   Clarence Birdseye freezes his last pea.

1962   Andy Warhol paints Norma Jean Baker.

1963   Lyndon Johnson becomes President. Aides spend six months trying to teach him how to pronounce 'negro'. They fail.

1964   Beatles' first invasion of the USA.

1965   New York City blacked out by power cut. Thousands pregnant.

1968   It is announced that many male criminals have an extra Y chromosome. Nixon is elected.

1969   A younger Kennedy drives off Chappaquiddick Bridge. *Oh Calcutta* comes to Broadway.

1970   A great cultural year: *MASH*, *Love Story*, and *Everything You Always Wanted to Know About Sex But were Afraid to Ask*.

1972   Baseball allows women umpires. Nixon re-elected.

1974   Ford pardons Nixon. Streaking becomes commonplace.

1976   53 per cent of US high school kids make it with marijuana. J. Paul Getty makes his last buck.

1977   *Star Wars* and Voyager 1 and 2 compete for popular acclaim.

1979   Norse penny dated 1065 found in Maine – left by Leif Erikson?

From 1980 on: Write your own history, folks.

ALL YOU NEED TO KNOW ABOUT BRITISH HISTORY

Moving back east, British history, as everyone knows, begins with the Roman invasion (55 BC, with continuous occupation from AD 43 to 407). The next date (a few battles and centuries of Viking pillage notwithstanding) is 1066, the Battle of Hastings when the Normans successfully invaded from France. Then came something called the Middle Ages and a bad King called John (1199–1216) who was forced to sign a declaration of human rights, the Magna Carta, which was not a bad first draft of the American Bill of Rights. After that, for some centuries, the history is of various kings and battles with all and every country round about (including English

versus Scots, a series of bloody civil wars that went on till as
late as 1745). Key monarchs to remember include Henry VIII
(1509–1547) who had not eight but six wives; Elizabeth I
(1558–1603) who put her cousin the Scottish claimant to
the English throne, Mary Queen of Scots, to death and in
whose reign much of North America (Raleigh, Drake, etc.)
was discovered; Charles I (1625–1649) who was beheaded
by Oliver Cromwell, the so-called Lord Protector, who led
Britain for its only republican period to 1659; George III
(1760–1820) who carelessly lost the American Colonies; Nelson and Wellington who defeated Napoleon; and Victoria
(1837–1901) the first monarch to be named after an age (or
possibly a railway station).

Now here are the key dates:

5000 BC	Britain's insularity begins. Continent cut off.
55 BC	Caesar visits Britain for first time.
AD 43	Romans (a sort of classically educated Mafia in togas) invade. As Heinrich Heine said, 'The Romans would never have had time to conquer the world if they'd had to learn Latin first.'
60	Boadicea or Boudicca, if you want to be authentic – an early version of Mrs T. – revolting.
196	North Britain overrun by Barbarians. People south of Watford say, 'Nothing's changed.'
787	Vikings start rape and pillage of Britain.
871	Alfred the Great burns some cakes.
1016	Canute tries to stop the tide coming in.
1066	William the Conqueror kills King Harold at Senlac Hill, not in Hastings.
1381	Wat Tyler (an early Arthur Scargill) leads Peasants' Revolt.

1436   Brewing of that warm, flat, brown liquid known
          as British beer first recorded.

1439   Kissing made illegal. Footballers go on strike.

1457   First golf match played in Scotland. King James
          II bans it because it distracts his men from ar-
          chery and thus is a threat to national defence.

1476   Caxton starts printing. (His presses are still, in-
          termittently, in daily use in Fleet Street.)

1492   England invades France. Retaliation for early
          Golden Delicious imports.

1496   Scotland invades England.

1517   First recorded mention of Scotch whisky. The
          English start drinking coffee.

1524   Londoners start using soap.

1525   Londoners stop using soap. (An Australian opi-
          nion.)

1536   Henry VIII starts Dissolution of Monasteries and
          executes the second of his six wives. (Note: His
          armour sports the biggest codpiece of any in the
          Tower of London.)

1539   Dutch cabbage introduced from the Netherlands.

1551   First recorded divorce (except of course for Henry
          VIII's). The grounds are adultery. Pubs start
          being licenced.

1577   Drake starts discovering the world, and chunks
          of America en route.

1583   Life Insurance Policies first issued. Salesmen
          complain they'll have to wait 300 years to start
          pestering prospective victims by telephone.

1586	American potatoes imported to Britain. The British start using forks.
1605	Guy Fawkes fails to blow up Parliament.
1609	Tea introduced. (Later to be re-exported to Boston.)
1625	King James bans smoking, on health and social grounds.
1633	Britain discovers bananas.
1642	England has its Civil War. Hairstyles become important.

1647	Newspaper advertising begins. Use of a tooth-brush first recorded.
1653	Britain goes Republican. Izaak Walton writes a book on fishing.
1660	Restoration of the (non-democratic) monarchy. Theatres open in celebration.
1666	London burns.
1674	Reports of the first game of billiards.
1686	Weather forecasting begins. A hot summer brings the first reported British sighting of an ice cream.
1694	Bank of England founded by a Scot.
1702	The Queen goes racing and encourages sweep-stakes.
1707	Great Britain incorporated.
1727	Rules of cricket drawn up by the Duke of Richmond. Many take to drinking gin as an alternative.
1747	First VD clinic opens. Handkerchiefs manufactured in Scotland.
1748	Cricket made legal. Increase in gin consumption noted.
1754	Golf club founded at St Andrews.
1762	First sandwich spread. Britain captures Cuba.
1805	Nelson wins, comes out of the closet, kisses Hardy and dies at the Battle of Trafalgar.
1818	Frankenstein invented by a woman.
1829	First Oxford and Cambridge Boat Race. Robert Peel invents the Police.

1837   Queen Victoria comes to the throne to Rule Britannia. Worcestershire Sauce goes on the market.

1843   Dickens publishes *A Christmas Carol*, Wordsworth is appointed Poet Laureate, and the *News of the World* begins publication. In short, a mixed year for the arts.

1847   First double-decker bus built.

1849   William Hamilton attempts to assassinate Queen Victoria. (No, not *that* Willie Hamilton.)

1852   First public lavatory opens in Fleet Street. Print workers relieved.

1859   Big Ben starts striking.

1865   Lord Palmerston says: 'Die, my good doctor? That's the *last* thing I shall do.'

1874   Winston Churchill is born of an American mother in a ladies' cloakroom. Britain annexes Fiji.

1877   Queen Victoria becomes Empress of India and is not amused when Darwin writes that he has discovered sex in plants.

1878   Britain occupies Cyprus, fights Afghanistan, Russia, etc. and invents the sugar cube.

1883   Karl Marx enters into another underground Communist plot at Highgate Cemetery.

1896   First motorist is convicted of speeding – at about 8 mph. *Daily Mail* has its first exclusive.

1900   First massage parlour opened. Ladysmith relieved. Old Etonians invent an old school tie.

1901   Elgar composes '*Pomp and Circumstance*'. Queen
        Victoria dies.

1909   Perms first come to London. Old Age Pensioners
        get theirs.

1910   Best-selling mousetrap invented in Leeds (not
        the Agatha Christie version, which arrived in
        1952).

1910   Dr Crippen (an American) is hanged in Britain
        for murdering his wife.

1914   Shaw writes *Pygmalion*. First World War opens.

1918   Armistice signed. Women get vote.

1919   American becomes first sitting British woman
        MP.

1920   Beer mats introduced.

1925   Two American imports, the Charleston and the
        Crossword, become crazes in Britain.

1926   General Strike. An anonymous worshipper puts
        a £1,000 banknote into the collection at Salis-
        bury Cathedral.

1933   First (sober, photographed) sighting of the Loch
        Ness Monster.

1936   King Edward abdicates in favour of his American
        wife.

1939   Daphne du Maurier publishes *Rebecca*. War de-
        clared.

1940   John Lennon born during an air raid and is
        christened Winston.

1941   Paul McCartney born. Clothes rationing intro-
        duced.

1943   Cilla Black is born Priscilla White. Monty fights at El Alamein.

1945   Orwell publishes *Animal Farm*. Labour government elected.

1946   Britain's first bikini sighted at Newquay. *Brief Encounter* screened.

1948   Bread rationing ends. First supermarket opens.

1950   US soccer team defeats England 1–0 in the World Cup.

1951   Witchcraft Act repealed. Black Magic now legal, but Milk Tray outlawed. Rowntrees celebrate.

1953   The Queen is crowned.

1954   Bill Haley and his Comets are worshipped.

1956   British Government invades Suez and abolishes third class rail travel.

1958   The first motorway opens and parking meters are introduced in Mayfair.

1961   Fruit-flavoured yoghurt introduced.

1964   Harold Wilson becomes PM and the Great Train Robbers get their desserts.

1966   Mini-skirts and ring-pull cans are introduced.

1970   Edward Heath becomes Prime Minister and the Beatles fall apart.

1973   Britain rejoins Europe. Britten composes *Death in Venice*.

1974   First McDonald's opens in London.

1979   Margaret Hilda Thatcher becomes first woman Prime Minister. Elton John leaves for Moscow.

From 1980 on: As above.

ENVOI

Thus the key elements of British and American history. In terms of bilateral relations, beyond recalling that Oscar Wilde on arriving in America in 1882 declared to the US Customs that he had 'nothing to declare but my genius', that Coca Cola was first imported into the UK in 1909 and the yo-yo in 1932, that the US added insult to the injury of the Boston Tea Party by interfering with Britain's national drink and introducing teabags in 1952, and that President Reagan complained to Mrs Thatcher that '... if only your people had come across the other ocean, the nation's capital would be in California', you now have it all.

4
A Common Language

"

An Englishman's way of speaking absolutely classifies him.
The moment he talks he makes some other Englishman despise him.

Alan Jay Lerner, *My Fair Lady*

One of the hardest languages for an American to learn is English.

RUSSELL BAKER

The British capitalize on their accent when they don't want you to know what they are saying. But if you wake them up at 4 am they speak perfect English, the same as we do.

HENRY KISSINGER

When the American people get through with the English language, it will look as if it had been run over by a musical comedy.

FINLAY PETER DUNNE, *Mr Dooley*

We speak American.

Bond Street shop sign

English spoken.

New York City shop sign

"

One of the advantages of trying to converse in Anglo-American is that your basic Anglo-American doesn't have to shout to make himself understood as he has to in, say, France or Germany. None the less, David Frost has etched in his memory his first encounter with the truth of George Bernard Shaw's (or Oscar Wilde's) dictum that we still are two nations divided by a common language. When he was completing one of the first TW3's in New York, he began to congratulate a guest by giving him the ultimate British compliment. 'Boffo,' he said, 'your piece went like a bomb.' The guest star dropped into instant dejection, since the word 'bomb' has precisely the opposite meaning Stateside. When Frost recounted the story later to Randolph Churchill, he understood immediately. 'Yes,' he said, 'and they have another word for disaster in America – 'to lay an egg'. Now, I would have thought that laying an egg was a good and natural thing for a hen to do. But not over there. ...' Quite what the reasoning behind all this is remains unclear, though obviously there must be a deep-seated linguistic antipathy towards our feathered friends in the States since the word 'turkey' is also used to define a bomb which has laid several of the above-mentioned eggs.

On another occasion Frost received a rave review for a special under a headline which was intended to be equally complimentary. The actual words, however, were 'DAVID FROST SPECIAL SLICK, SCHMALTZY AND INGRATIATING' – which seemed a bitter blow. But in the US 'slick' means polished – not glib – 'schmaltzy' implies heart rather than saccharin, and 'ingratiating' indicates an admirable desire to please rather than an unwelcome bout of sycophancy.

Foreigners, i.e. non-English speaking people, often are more aware of the differences than we Anglo-Americans. Thus the West German Embassy in London recently received a booklet from Bonn entitled *Germany's Contribution to Western Defense*. Inside was an explanatory slip which said, in German: 'This book has been written in American English. Nevertheless, we believe it will be readily understandable by the British.' They appreciate only too well that there are other dangerously

I suppose once you've mastered the grammar...

total opposites. To enjoin in the UK is to encourage: to enjoin in the US is to forbid by law. A public school in the UK means what is called a private school in the US. (Senior pupils at public schools in the UK also have younger boys as their own personal fags as well, but that's another story.) And beware in negotiations; if you table a point in the UK you propose it for immediate discussion; if you table it in the States, you are seeking to delay the discussion for an unspecified amount of time. Michael Shea's key test of how well an expat American is doing in London is to ask: 'Is a lady barrister without her briefs a solicitor?'

Then there are other simple differences of vocabulary. We all know that in the journey from the States to the UK, a sidewalk on Main Street becomes a pavement on the High Street. Sneakers become plimsolls or trainers, checkers become draughts, the first floor becomes the ground floor and the second floor becomes the first floor and so on; logically, newly liberated Englishmen should come out of the cupboard rather than the closet. A station wagon turns into an estate car, the trunk of the car becomes its boot (though beware of the British expression, 'to put the boot in' – i.e., to attack someone in a particularly ruthless way). The hood (US) becomes another piece of headgear in Britain, the bonnet – but in the UK 'hood' means the soft top of a convertible. In the journey from the UK to the States, jumble sales become garage sales, coffins become caskets, shares lodged at a merchant bank become stocks at an investment bank, dressing gowns become bathrobes, dinner jackets become tuxedos, vests go from being underwear to outerwear, trousers become pants, pants become shorts and shorts become drinks. And, inexplicably, green fingers turn into green thumbs.

For the American visiting London there are various pitfalls. If he wants to stay in an apartment, he should call it a flat. He should also beware of seeking to stay in a co-op because, if successful, he would find himself dossing down on the floor of a down-market chain of department stores.

If he ventures out to buy food he will want tins rather than cans, sweets rather than candy, salt beef rather than corned beef (which here is a quite different product in tins), fish soup rather than chowder, crisps rather than chips, chips rather than fries, biscuits rather than cookies, jam rather than jelly and jelly rather than jello. At the end of a meal in a restaurant he will want a bill rather than a check, and a toilet rather than a bathroom (on which see a separate section below). He will find English muffins almost as little known as a national delicacy as French fries are known as such in France or as Danish pastries in Denmark.

There are a number of dos and don'ts. As you clutch your carrier bag (not tote bag) of duty frees, don't tell the Customs man that you are the proud possessor of a Purple Heart, or you will be arrested for possession of an illegal amphetamine pill. Don't ask for seats in the orchestra, unless you are really proficient with a French horn (known in France as an English horn). Do remember that a dame may not be a broad in the Damon Runyon sense of the word but an ennobled seventy-six-year-old female ex-civil servant. And a reference to those beautiful broads is likely to be equally unerotic – just a description of a group of lakes and canals in the east of England. Don't talk too much about imitating your peer group: people may think you're name-dropping about sixteen members of the House of Lords. Again, many years ago, before the authors met, Shea asked a friend of Frost's: 'How do you find him?' He was rewarded with the latter's telephone number.

Don't tell your hostess you want to go and bathe before dinner – she will show you the local municipal swimming baths. And if you are surveying the political scene, remember that state control means the reverse of what it does in the US – more centralization rather than less – and that an MP is a Member of Parliament not a military policeman. And talking of MPs, you will find they do not run for office like political candidates in the States – they stand for a seat. And when you watch them in action you may decide that is a pretty perceptive comment on the relative vigour of the two sets of politicians.

And beware the word 'fanny' – in the UK it traditionally refers to the front and not the back (though we are becoming corrupted). When asked to explain how she kept her wonderful figure, a New York lady friend of the authors electrified a London dinner party at attributing everything to the way she went back and forth across the living room on her fanny ten times a day. Every English woman present winced visibly.

However, most of the problems for Americans in England are, as you can see, eminently manageable. The linguistic problems for the Englishman abroad in the States are somewhat more fraught. It starts on a relatively minor level. 'Can I help you wash up?' will bewilder an American who thinks he is being accused of an incapacity to wash himself, but it soon gets more serious. Do not, for example, compliment your host on the welcome you received by saying, 'Your wife is so

homely.' That says not warm, but ugly. 'Mean' now says unkind rather than stingy, and 'neat' becomes excellent rather than tidy. And watch out for these little changes in homespun advice that can be so valuable. Michael Shea remembers realizing, in show time, that an American friend was trying to be kind with his remark: 'Never stand between a dog and a fire hydrant, Mike.' For fire hydrant, read lamp post, and just hope it's not too late.

The proud and husky rugby player should not declaim, 'I work in a bank but what I really enjoy is being a hooker.' Female visitors should not exult over the joys back home of playing with their pussies, and neither male nor female visitors should exhort their host to keep his pecker up, however inspirational that might sound in the UK. (Thus President Johnson's 'I never trust a man unless I've got his pecker in my pocket.') Michael Shea also remembers a curious silence when he referred to a lady having a ladder in her tights. It took time to explain that this was no strange sexual deviation but a mere run in her pantyhose. And remember a cock is a rooster, and the verb 'to hump' means a good deal more than 'to carry something heavy'.

America is, in short, a minefield of potential hazard for the visiting Brit. The excitement of watching John McEnroe should not be encapsulated by stating, 'He really gave me a bang.' The English maiden who enters a stationer's and asks for a rubber in case of her making a mistake may well be redirected to a pharmacy, though not to a condominium. (The correct word would be 'eraser'.) Any lady who says she's very good at French may get more attention than she feels is warranted. And of course the apocryphal English matron who, newly arrived in New York, called the bell captain and asked him ever so reasonably to knock her up at eight o'clock in the morning, got a form of room service she wasn't entirely anticipating.

It's all quite confusing. That's for our American readers. For our British readers, it's all very confusing. Which, translating once again, means it's totally confusing for everybody.

And two last tips for the unwary:

For Britons: many Americans, of all classes, are capable of irony.

For Americans: many Britons, even from the upper classes, are capable of sincerity.

WORD AVOIDANCE

IN THE UK

The following is a list of words which the English find amusing – whoever says them and whatever the context. Teams of semanticists have laboured fruitlessly for years to discover why. If you sense one of these words approaching in your conversation, use a synonym. If no synonym suggests itself, leave the room immediately pleading sudden nausea.

Rissoles	Rice pudding	Blancmange
Rhubarb	String vest	Marshmallow
Wart	Lard	Hernia
Wick	Carbuncle	Rabbi
Budgie	Gout	Toffees
Piccalilli	Girdle	Yodelling
Gherkin	Knock knees	Whippet
Vole	Vest	Nightie
Knickers	Mother-in-law	Brussel sprouts
Kilt	Fish fingers	Parrot
Wooden leg	Whelks	Cockles
Ear Trumpet	Tripe	Winkles
Corsets	Sprats	Prune
Aspidistra	Wedding night	Gabbitas & Thring
Trouser leg	Buttocks	Budleigh Salterton
Cock	Falsies/false teeth	

IN THE U S

In recent years a similar trend has been emerging in America. Travellers should beware that the following words already have the same effect in the United States as those listed above have in England. Our advice remains the same. Americans will be unable not to laugh at the following:

Hemorrhoids	Beaver	Chopped liver
Zits	Belly Button	Psoriasis
Pissant	John	Prune Danish
Newark	Prosthesis	Third leg
Bosom	Smelts	Butt

Poontang	Snatch	Tush
Hanky	Pickle	Head
Wiener	Philbert	Goitre

ARCHAIC EXPRESSIONS OF ASTONISHMENT

Amazed English people no longer say:

Zounds!	Blimey O'Reilly!
By Jove!	Lor luvaduck!
By Jupiter!	Lawks-a-mercy!
Deuce take you!	Cor blimey!
Confound it!	What the blazes!
Great snakes!	Wizard prang!
'Pon my soul!	Absolutely spiffing!
As I live and breathe!	Awfully nice weather!
By heavens!	Jolly good show!
Great powers!	Everybody out!
Hang it!	Pip! Pip!
What the deuce!	

Amazed Americans no longer say:

Well, I'm a monkey's uncle!	I'll be a ring-tailed polecat!
The heck you say!	Land's sakes!
Gee willikins!	Sassafras!
Gosh sakes!	Suffering seaweed!
Tarnation!	Well, strip my gears and call me shiftless!
Goldurnit!	
Dang bust it!	Well, dial me and call me phoney!
Godfrey Daniel!	

Further note: archaic expressions of delight Americans no longer use:

Groovy, man!	Super-dooper!
Real cool!	Heavy!
That's boss!	Outta sight!
Like wow!	I'm gone!
Solid!	Neat-o!
That sends me!	Keen-o!

Even more archaic (pre-1960) exclamations of delight that Americans no longer use:

Swell!	Bet your sweet potootie!
Gosharoonie!	Yippie-ay-o!

Expressions of delight that Americans *do* use:

You mean you take Visa, Mastercard, *and* American Express?!

THE SPELLING GAME

A heavy debate, laden with entrenched prejudice on both sides (if you can load an entrenched prejudice) continues, it is said, in etymological circles, about the differences in spelling of the same words both sides of the great watery divide. We are certainly not going to argue the case as to which is right or better, but it's useful to have a few of the obvious examples. Among the most common are:

English	*American*
Centre	Center
Programme	Program
Through	Thru
Tomato	Tomáto

Aluminium	Aluminum
Kerb	Curb
Tyre	Tire
Theatre	Theater
Aeroplane	Airplane
Labour	Labor
Neighbour	Neighbor
Savour	Savor

In general, for sheer economy of letters – average 12 per cent in the examples above – the United States reigns supreme. For visitors from one country to another, the message is clear: watch your Rs.

RHYMING SLANG

We cannot overstate the importance to Americans visiting the United Kingdom of developing a command of 'rhyming slang'. Suddenly, without warning, the moment will come when you are forced to employ it in your conversation. When this moment will come cannot be predicted – except to say that it won't be while you are in England because, apart from a few exceptions, rhyming slang is not generally part of everyday conversation in the British Isles.

No, the moment when it *will* be needed will be when you have returned to America and your friends and relatives demand a demonstration of it as the price for being forced to look at your holiday slides. This, then, is one foreign language you can learn on the plane home. Here are a few examples:

Errol Flynn	chin
Vera Lynn	gin
Vera and Philharmonic	gin and tonic
Gregory Peck	cheque
False alarms	arms
Lillian Gish	fish
Lilley and Skinner	dinner
Lord Mayor	swear
Dog and bone	phone
Farmer Giles	piles
Half-inch	pinch
Mince pies	eyes
Boat race	face
Dickie dirt	shirt
Adam and Eve	believe
Ice-cream freezer	geezer (gent)

Beware also a local refinement whereby the English sometimes use only the first non-rhyming word of a two-word slang term:

Butcher's (hook)	look
Barnet (Fair)	hair
Plates (of meat)	feet
Bristol (City)	titty
Whistle (and flute)	suit
On your Tod (Sloan)	alone

However, when you're talking to your fellow Americans, feel free to invent your own rhyming slang. Since there is no authoritative guide, no one will feel able to contradict you. Or, as we *might* say in England, 'Since there is no authoritative *slip'n* (slip'n'slide = guide) no one will feel *kitchen* (kitchen table = able) to *pogo* (pogosticked = contradict) you.' Try it and *housewives*! (Housewives' knee = see).

THE LANGUAGE OF LOVE

Whose love is given over-well
Shall look on Helen's face in hell,
While they whose love is thin and wise
May view John Knox in Paradise.

DOROTHY PARKER

In Great Britain	*In America*
The scene: a bar. He will introduce himself by saying:	
'Cheer up – it may never happen!'	'Hey. What's happenin'?'
To which she will reply:	
'I think it just has!'	'Not much!'
He'll persuade her to furnish him with her phone number in order that he may:	
'Give her a tinkle.'	'Call her up.'

And say:

'Er, I wondered if you   'Let's do lunch.'
were by chance free for,
er, a, um, lunch some
time this week?'

Not too many lunches later, there develops:

'A mad pash'.   'A mash'.

He tells her she must know he's:

'Absolutely bonkers   'Got the hots for you', or
about you'.   'hot to trot'.

And she obviously thinks he's:

'Dishy'.   'Awesome'.

He will start calling her:

'poppet' or 'slinkybum'.   'hon' or 'toots' or 'sweetie'.

She will start calling him:

'froggie' or 'old bean'.   'big boy' or 'buster'.

And they will spend their weekends:

'sleeping with each other'.   'humping'.

She'll be delighted to tell her friends that he's:

'quite well off, actually'.   'loaded. We're talking
        megabucks here!'

*And he will not be above boasting to his friends that she has
terrific:*

'boobs'.   'jugs'.

If only they didn't row so much! The number of times he's told her to:

'put a sock in it'.   'bag your head'.

And she, in return, has told him to:

'shut your face'.   'zip your lip'.

No wonder he's decided she's a:

'stupid cow'.   'total bozo'.

And she's decided he's a:

'silly twit'.   'schmuck'.

Frankly they're both:

'fed up to the back teeth'   'pissed off'.
– or, indeed, 'pissed off'.

And find each other a pain in the:

'neck' or 'arse'.   'butt' or 'ass'.

Time, obviously, to give each other:

'the boot'.   'the kiss-off'.

And go out and get:

'thoroughly slaughtered'.   'totally ripped'.

MID-ATLANTIC SLANG

New words are often coined on the transatlantic route. Many gradually enter the language. The current contenders for such elevation are:

transic, *n.*   One of the vast majority of constant transatlantic travellers. A dull dog who does not relish nor seek out the jetsetter lifestyle. Wears business suits for travelling. The aeroplane is just an extension of his office, and he works throughout the journey.

midat (or mydat), *n.* (pronounced 'my-dat')   One of those people who are totally **bipatrisan** (*sic*), i.e., completely at home on either side of the Atlantic. It's impossible to tell where they bought their clothes, luggage, cologne, etc. Their accents will be **midat** (*adj.*) too.

dovate, *v.*   To cultivate, as of stewardesses. Also: **dovation**, the art of stewardess cultivation. (Unlike the man who snapped his fingers repeatedly at a stewardess for attention only to be told, 'It takes more than two fingers to make me come.') **Midats dovate** well and always get most attention, their drinks first, etc.

pearl, *v.*   To be in a state of suspension of effort and time brought about by frequent transatlantic travel. Thus: 'He was still pearling when he got home and consequently forgot it was his wife's birthday, to help with the dishes, change the baby's nappy, etc., etc.'

grud, *n.*   A transatlantic traveller who looks and behaves like a tramp. He and his many items of hand baggage overspill into your seat or, if he's in the seat in front of you, he's the one who decides to recline his seat just as you are about to write a letter or have dinner.

prink, *n.*   The sort of person who sits beside you on an aircraft and insists on talking or telling you his life story throughout the entire journey. Expert **transics** know how to deal with this: e.g., by wearing headsets throughout, switched to a silent channel. **Gruds** are often also **prinks**. **Dovate** neither.

5
Social Institutions

"

'It is in bad taste' is the most formidable word
an Englishman can pronounce.

EMERSON

The English winter – ending in July,
To recommence in August.'

BYRON, *Don Juan*

Walking is an un-American activity.

LORD KINROSS

In England, if something goes wrong – say if
one finds a skunk in the garden – he writes to
the family solicitor who proceeds to take the
proper measures; whereas in America you telephone the fire department. Each satisfied a
characteristic need: in the English, love of
order and legalistic procedures; and here in
America what you like is something vivid, and
red and swift.

ALFRED NORTH WHITEHEAD

(*Authors' note*: Skunks are rare in English gardens, but
who are we to quibble with ANW?)

"

Isn't he adorable? He belongs to our American guests. Say "hi", Wilmer.

BED AND BREAKFAST IF YOU CAN STAND IT

Americans are much in awe of British social institutions. This is exemplified by the much varied story of a bewigged and resplendent Lord Chancellor Hailsham, processing in all grandeur through the corridors of the Houses of Parliament and spotting his good friend Neil Martin, MP. Remembering that it was the latter's birthday, he called out, 'Neil!' Whereupon, a group of totally overawed, blue-rinsed American tourists did just that. A less impressed American told an MP on one occasion that hypocrisy was the Vaseline of British social intercourse, which led to an unseemly little row and the less subtle riposte, 'God must love stupid Americans. He made so many of them.' Peace fell eventually.

BRITISH/AMERICAN INSTITUTIONAL EQUIVALENTS

The process of adjustment to the transatlantic culture shock is assisted by a certain amount of prior indoctrination. Thus a totally partial, biased, highly selective list of roughly equivalent institutions such as that which follows can be a useful tool in terms of instant mid-Atlantic one-upmanship. Each equivalent (so-called) really requires pages of qualification which would only confuse, which is why we do not provide it. Thus we have:

American	British
The Senate	The House of Lords
The House of Representatives	The House of Commons
Johnny Carson	Terry Wogan
Congress	Parliament
The White House	Buckingham Palace plus 10 Downing Street
J. R. Ewing	J. R. Ewing
Wall Street	The City (of London)
Broadway	Drury Lane/Shaftesbury Avenue
Saks	Harrods
—	Mrs Thatcher
The Village	Chelsea
The Statue of Liberty	A mix of Nelson's Column and the White Cliffs of Dover
Alcatraz	Dartmoor
CIA	MI6
Diners	Transport Caffs
FBI/Secret Service	MI5/Special Branch
The Kentucky Derby (pron Durby)	The Derby (pron Darby)
President Reagan	—
The Secretary of State	The Foreign (and Commonwealth) Secretary
The Treasury Secretary	The Chancellor of the Exchequer
42nd Street NYC beyond 5th	Soho (the seamy side)
The State Department	The Foreign Office

The AFL/CIO	The TUC
PX	NAAFI
West Point	Sandhurst
Richard Nixon	(Name removed at request of Publishers)
Annapolis	Dartmouth
Amtrak	British Rail
Superbowl	FA Cup Final
Ann Landers	Claire Rayner
AT & T	British Telecom
Peoplexpress	Virgin Atlantic
Disneyland	Alton Towers
National Lampoon (not *True Detective*)	*Private Eye*
Internal Revenue	Inland Revenue
The Mason–Dixon Line	See 'North of Watford'

SOCIAL INSTITUTIONS: AN A TO Z

A society, we aver, is trademarked both by the character of its people and by its institutions. We have already summarized the national characteristics of the Americans and the British, which was a difficult, highly questionable and dangerous game, since just as each individual's perception of another is highly subjective, so much more is an individual country's view of its neighbour.

With institutions we may be on scarcely safer ground. Let us look at a haphazard, non-exclusive, totally subjective selection, arranged alphabetically.

A BRITISH A TO Z

Aldershot Home of the British Army. The signs for Aldershot Camp should thus not be taken as a British equivalent of West Hollywood. It is known for the following popular railway graffito: 'Passengers are requested not to use the toilet while the train is standing at a station – except at Aldershot.'

Ascot   Horse racing and women's hats. One of the most certain places to see members of the Royal Family, and Britain's most distinguished gossip columnists.

Auchtermuchty   The Oshkosh, Wisconsin of Scotland.

Barmaids   They work in pubs and serve pints and if formed in the traditional mould they are blonde, buxom and of uncertain age. They are unshockable listeners to countless dubious stories and tales of woe. They are purveyors of laughter and advice with every pint pulled and are also ready with a steadying half-nelson (a wrestling term: an arm lock on the neck) should you overstep the mark.

Ben Nevis   As the highland dominie (teacher) said, 'It's the highest mountain in the world [4,406 ft] ... except of course for those in foreign parts.'

Blackpool   Atlantic City without the gambling and the Mob, though Blackpool landladies can be just as frightening.

Boat Race   An annual rowing race between the Oxford and Cambridge University teams (eight in each boat plus a cox – the person who steers) which takes place on the River Thames from Putney to Mortlake, usually in March, and which has taken place for the last 130-odd years. To enjoy the race requires the same sort of special enthusiasm as is required for watching cricket (q.v.) or old ladies knitting.

Bognor Regis   A seaside town of which it has been said, 'If I could chose a place to die, I would choose Bognor: the transition from life would hardly be noticeable.'

Cambridge

> For Cambridge people rarely smile,
> Being urban, squat and full of guile.
> Rupert Brooke

Chelsea Flower Show A must for garden lovers if you don't mind queueing to see each and every flower.

Constitutional (usually early morning) The English are walking enthusiasts. If you are trying it, remember before crossing the street, 'Look right – not left.' It's fun – and it's informative.

Country weekend The grander variety can be traumatic for a sensitive bachelor – trying to stuff bits of tissue paper in shirts and trousers so that it looks as though you hadn't done it yourself. One American student we know was taken aside by the butler in a very grand house who said, 'I'm sorry, sir, I'm afraid your man forgot to pack your brushes.'

Darts Pub games most played north of Watford. Unwritten rules appear to stipulate one round (of drinks) for one round (of darts).

Establishment A term probably born, certainly developed, in the mid-1950s. It is, in the words of Henry Fairlie, 'the matrix of official and social relations with which power is exercised'. A sort of modified top people's club.

Fawkes (Guy) A commemoration is held on 5 November every year of the man who failed to blow up the House of Commons, by burning on a bonfire a 'guy' or stuffed effigy representing Mr Fawkes as his eternal punishment for trying to raise the level of Parliament.

Fog Old reputations die hard. Fog died out in the UK (except at Heathrow) following the 1956 Clean Air Act and 'pea-soupers' are long a thing of the past, living on only in

American television movies based on the works of Charles Dickens.

Gloucestershire   The uppermost country county, populated mainly by the Royal Family at weekends and retired professional cricketers.

Glyndebourne   Britain's poshest picnic. Get some well-heeled friend to take you to this opera in a garden.

Graffiti   A proud English cultural tradition. All modern graffiti are based on one of three traditional examples. Post-War advertising hoardings always bore the warning, 'Bill Stickers will be prosecuted.' Which led to the addition by graffitologists, 'Bill Stickers is innocent.' Or, 'Bill Stickers is innocent, OK?' Equally famous was the inscription, 'I love grils.' Which led to the addition, 'You mean girls, stupid.' Which in turn led to the later addition, 'What about us grils?' Equally important in the development of this new art form was, 'My mother made me a homosexual', which brought the response, 'If I give her the wool will she make me one too?' As a result the industry expanded to 'Procrastinate now', and 'I like sadism, necrophilia and bestiality. Am I flogging a dead horse?' If you see a sign saying, 'Keep Britain tidy – kill a tourist', do not be alarmed. It's just another joke (we think).

Harrogate   Not a British version of Watergate set in a public school, but a spa where political parties behave almost as badly at their annual conferences.

Harwich   One of the gateways to Europe. Source of another famous graffiti: 'Harwich for the Continent – Paris for the incontinent.'

Hogmanay (New Year's Eve)   A Scottish festival mainly devoted to 'seeing the New Year in', to the accompaniment of vast amounts of locally distilled amber firewater known as whisky. (NB: 'Scotch' is the purely American term for Scottish whisky. In Scotland whisky is always Scotch and never Bourbon, let alone whiskey with an 'e', which is the Irish version. In short, always ask for a whisky if it's a Scotch you want. If

you want ice with it, particularly in Scotland, you have to
order it specially. There are lots of simple ethnic jokes about
catching cold if you dilute it with water as well.)

Irish stew   What Britain seems perpetually to be in.

John Bull   From his top hat to his Union Jack waistcoat, the
Englishman's idea of what God must look like in his street
clothes.

Kirk   The Church of Scotland which, in its most extreme
form, is a strict and intolerant organization whose elders are
constantly tormented by the suspicion that someone, somewhere in Scotland, may be shamelessly enjoying himself.

Lawns   Unsurpassed anywhere in the world. As the old gar-
dener said in answer to an enquiry, 'Plant it, then simply cut
it and roll it for a couple of hundred years...'

Letters to The Times   The sounding board for the British
Establishment. Popular topics include legal safeguards for
hedgehogs and the price of snuff, and there is an annual one,
always from the same person and eagerly awaited, about the
most popular names for children as recorded in the birth
columns of that newspaper.

Lloyds of London   Currently under a cloud (for which they
are not insured).

McMafia   The top Scots who run large sectors of British life.

Monarchy   A subject of much study by Fleet Street. The
monarchy as a non-party symbol of national unity was de-
cisively rejected by the United States in 1776. Since then,
Britain has had many kings and queens although, as commentators pointed out at the time, under President Kennedy,
the United States did at least have a jack.

Morris dancing   The 'traditional' English country dance. Seldom seen, supposedly enjoyable to participate in, stultifying
to watch.

Motorways   Which are always under repair thus necessitating 'contraflow' systems. When sitting in a ten-mile two-lane tailback, remember the law: the other queue always moves faster – unless you change lanes.

National (Grand)   The world's premier steeplechase. This difficult and treacherous four-and-a-half mile race involves thirty jumps including the legendary Beecher's Brook, and a large field of experienced horses, several of whom finish.

Oban   Town on the west coast of Scotland, at the same latitude as Nain, Labrador. Palm trees grow in profusion here, an indication of the beneficial effects of the Gulf Stream. There's one outside the town hall and another outside the post office.

Old boy network   Part of the British way of life whereby old school chums run those parts of British life not run by the McMafia.

Perthshire   A sort of Scottish Gloucestershire with raspberries and a dubious amount of kilt-weaving.

Plymouth   As in Brethren. Currently renowned as a stronghold of the co-head of the government in exile, by name one Dr David Owen.

Quaint   An intended compliment that will invariably backfire. Remarking to a Brit, 'Gee, that's just so quaint' will be about as welcome as warmly referring to a freedom fighter as a terrorist.

Repairmen   Gas, electricity, and domestic appliance repairmen arrive, seldom if ever on time, bearing the wrong tools, few spare parts and expressions of total pessimism. When shown the faulty item, they always respond with a sharp intake of breath.

Rugby   A school and a rather tough game. Visit the first: do not play the second as it is a game played by Welshmen and gentlemen with odd-shaped balls.

Sloane Rangers   Adult English preppies, also known as 'the green-wellie brigade' (wellies = Wellingtons, q.v., and green ones are *de rigueur* country wear).

Snooker   A national pastime that has begun rivalling cricket as the television-fuelled opium of the people.

Soho   The sex, strip, porn, clip joint and sleaze centre of London. A sad place. Once bohemian, now tacky.

Summer   As the poet Coleridge said, 'Summer has set in with its usual severity.' This happens each year around the beginning of June. In Britain it is a time for straw boaters (hats), punts (flat boats) on the river, the sound of leather on willow (cricket ball on bat), and old men on benches sipping cider or possibly pints of ale. For much of the time it rains.

Taxis   Always pay at the end of the journey once you are outside, and not through the partition as you would in the States.

Twelfth, the Glorious   Grouse shooting begins on 12 August. A grouse shot on 11 August gets *very* annoyed.

Unicorn   One of the supporters of the Royal Coat of Arms, a symbol of national pride and virility – thus the old French saying: 'Never play leapfrog with a unicorn.'

Upper lip, stiff   A facial peculiarity originally coinciding with assertions such as 'A ratio of three to one in Jerry's favour? Suits me, Sir!' And 'I've copped it in the back, Sir, but I'm still going to have a crack at the blighters!' Now more commonly associated with observations such as, 'I need you, Daphne, I never knew how much!' and 'Perhaps it's just as well, Felicity, if we never see each other again!'

VAT   VAT 69 is a leading whisky (or the Pope's telephone number). VAT is, less popularly, also Value Added Tax, a

sales tax. Americans may, incidentally, qualify for exemption
from VAT on goods exported. So when you make your larger
purchases of VAT 69, ask the shop assistant about VAT
'86.

Wellington   Home of the famous General, a public (i.e. private) school and a rubber boot. Also a sumptuous private
hospital in London, which only oil sheiks can afford.

Winchester   Rigorous academic school. Motto: 'Manners
Makyth Man'. Produces articulate men, often of socialist per-
suasion, and lawyers. Old boys (called Wykehamists) are intellectual, but (often terminally) unworldly.

Xenophobia   Traditional British fear or dislike of foreigners.
Broadly speaking, the British view is: If foreigners are really
intelligent, they'd speak English. Since Americans *do* speak
English, or at least make a reasonable stab at it, they will find
themselves made welcome by the average British xenophobe.

Yorkshire   Haunt of Yorkshiremen, a breed of men so xenophobic (see above) that they consider all other Englishmen
foreigners.

Zebra crossing   Black and white striped cross walks, marked
by poles with orange globes on top, at which most cars will
stop for pedestrians. Thus, policeman (to American trying
unsuccessfully to cross road): 'There's a zebra crossing just
round the corner, Sir?' American: 'I hope he's having more
success than I am.'

AN AMERICAN A TO Z

Air Conditioning   This has changed the South and made it
tolerable to work in over the last thirty or forty years. Elsewhere it is either too hot or too cold (usually both), especially
in hotel bedrooms. In Las Vegas you put on a sweater to go
indoors.

Baseball   American national pastime, though not necessarily its most popular sport. Play ends after nine innings, but even if one team is hopelessly behind, right until the end they still have a chance to come back and win – as in Mr Yogi Berra's famous saying, 'It ain't over 'til it's over.' Beware of the food. The much-celebrated ball park frank both looks and tastes like what a ball park frank sounds like.

Bermuda shorts   The most unflattering male garment ever produced, for which the United States rather than Bermuda must take the blame. The Bermuda Triangle pales by comparison.

Cabbies   'Help wanted' ads in NY papers claim you can get a cabby's licence in three days. Most people are surprised they have been driving that long.

Diets   Inventing diets is a great American pastime. This is followed, almost invariably, by the much-publicized publication of a best-selling book which will then alternate at the top of the best-seller lists with a book on how to save money and get rich during the build-up to Armageddon.

ERA   At a Manhattan cocktail party this means the Equal Rights Amendment. In a bar in Brooklyn the subject is probably baseball rather than women's consciousness-raising. Here ERA is earned run average.

Football   It's a savage business. Yes, they really do go out on the field and try to hurt the other players. Yes, players do get hurt. Yes, the men that hurt them continue to play. It is even more dangerous for the fans who park themselves in front of the tube with several cans of beer, chips and hyperthyroid sandwiches filled with carcinogenic substances and spend the afternoon watching at least two games back to back, switching stations to other games during the commercials. Definitely a health hazard.

Graffiti   A more robust style than the British equivalent, especially in New York: e.g. 'Texans are living proof that Indians screwed buffaloes.'

Hey, it could be a lot worse. You could be back home, eating a jellied eel.

At a cricket match.

Greyhound buses Long-distance coaches providing cheap, swift travel and the opportunity to meet the sort of Americans you don't meet in England. The Americans you meet in England, who fly everywhere, describe the Greyhound bus terminals as 'the armpit of America'. This is what they've heard and they're wrong. Things have changed. The only exceptions are the terminals in New York and Los Angeles, recently renamed 'Death Wish 4 and 5'.

Hall of Fame The only election in America that is truly based on personal merit and accomplishment.

Hangups

America has become so tense and nervous, it's been years since I've seen anyone asleep in church.

NORMAN VINCENT PEALE

Health clubs   Beginning to replace the singles bar. Designer shorts and leotards enhance the already-developed torso. Dates are made for dinner, movies or just a quiet evening of arm wrestling. NB: no smoking allowed, on the basis that smoking is one of the main causes of statistics.

Hockey (ice, not field)   Although traditionally associated with Canada, hockey has now become one of America's favourite team sports. Those familiar with the Olympic style of play may be a little put off by the rough and often crude brand of American professional hockey. At least one bare-fisted brawl breaks out during the game and after that, a patch of blood will stain the ice where the fight broke out. Apart from that, it's highly sporting (cf. Christians versus Lions).

Houseplants   Deprived of fresh air by universal air conditioning and of greenery by acid rain, city dwellers pack their houses with houseplants which they treat as Brits treat their dogs.

Insomnia   The whole country, at least in the cities, suffers from it. Shops, cinemas, clubs, news stands stay open all night. So if you're an insomniac, don't lose any sleep over it – go out and enjoy the facilities.

Jazz   Along with modern dance and Hollywood, jazz is America's major contribution to world culture. It came from Africa.

Ku Klux Klan   A secret organization of white Southerners who wear white sheets. Their hats have a point – which is more than can be said for their beliefs.

Lobbyists   There are really three political parties in the United States: the Democrats, the Republicans and the Lobbyists. Of the three, the latter are the most powerful.

Muhammad Ali   Few have commanded the attention and admiration of the entire sporting world more than Kentucky-born Cassius Clay who changed his 'slave name' to

Muhammad Ali. As one commentator said after one of his most graceful performances, 'There is no justice in the world. Why is it that the blacks have all the natural rhythm when it's the Catholics who really need it?'

NRA (National Rifle Association)   A major lobbying group opposed to gun control legislation. They believe that an American has as much right to bear arms as a Scotsman has to bare legs. And they usually have as little under their hats as the Scots have under their kilts.

Old Glory   The Stars and Stripes – the flag of the United States. A citizen of the United States is protected by the American flag in every country – except the United States.

Psychiatrists   Visitors to America will find that psychiatrists have a power in that land that they have nowhere else in the world. Apparently well-adjusted couples will only be happy when they can find something to go to a psychiatrist and be miserable about. Psychiatrists share a near monopoly of power in America with lawyers and lobbyists.

Quogue   A summer resort for fashionable New Yorkers situated on Long Island on the way to the Hamptons. If it's true that a little gossip goes a long way for New Yorkers in the summer, Quogue and the Hamptons are where it goes to.

Rupertmurdoch   A colloquial term or an expression of regret. Rupert's major contribution to American life thus far has been his development of the art of the headline. As we go to press, the two outstanding examples to date have been his *Boston Herald*, during Klaus von Bülow's trial for the attempted murder of his heiress wife, with 'MAID TO JURY: KLAUS WAS A LOUSE' and his *New York Post* with 'HEADLESS BODY FOUND IN TOPLESS BAR'.

Senior citizens   Most of them are rounded up and sent to Florida, where they won't cause any trouble to the cocaine dealers.

Size   A great American institutional preoccupation which it is difficult for the British to understand. Thus the tale of the gauche American student sitting opposite Noël Coward in a railway compartment and daring to open the conversation with a remark, 'Gee, I reckon ya could fit little old England into one corner of Nebraska.' Coward's languid reply: 'But to what point, young man?'

Subways (NYC)   The world's biggest psychiatric outpatient clinic. As someone said, 'The stairs, escalators and routes were all designed by Escher.' The subways make Beirut seem like Bournemouth.

Ten-gallon hats   Like many Western boasts, these only hold around a gallon.

Times Square   No war can be over, no New Year officially begun, until it has been celebrated in Times Square, with its famous neon billboards, now exclusively rented by Japanese film companies.

Uncle Sam   The personification of the United States. He's a white-haired, bearded gent, dressed in the Stars and Stripes and a tall hat – the latter being necessitated, American tax-payers suspect, by the fact that he's constantly passing it around.

Vacation   The American way of getting into the pink by going into the red.

Warning signs   There is something simple and direct about American warning signs, e.g., 'Wrong way' and 'Don't even think of parking here.' We also liked the airline steward's announcement just prior to take-off, 'If your destination is not Caspar, Wyoming, this would be a good moment to make this fact known to the cabin staff.'

Xmas   An annual pagan sales ritual which begins in October. Henry James said, 'An American woman who respects herself must buy something every day of her life.' Xmas allows her to fill in any gaps.

Yuppy   An American crossbreed, only recently identified and better known as a Young Urban Professional. The Yuppy loves jogging, sushi, Nikes, wine spritzers, American Express Gold Cards, pasta salads, caviar and – above all – the fact that so many books have been written about him and his pals. Not to be confused with Yappies (Young Aspiring Professionals) and Yumpies (Young Upwardly Mobile Professionals). There are also Guppies (Gay Urban Professionals) and Puppies (Pregnant Urban Professionals). Grumpies are Yuppies with job burnout, and Frumpies are ugly Yuppies. A Humpy is a Yuppy who hangs out in singles bars, where they're most likely to pick up a Herpy – which some feel is better than a Yuppy blind date: a Yucky.

Zip code   The American equivalent of Britain's Postcode. Every address in America is followed by its own zip code – with the exception of Lincoln's Gettysburg.

6
Politics

"

In America the President reigns for four years,
and journalism reigns for ever and ever.

OSCAR WILDE

All America has to do to get in bad all over
the world is just to start out on what we think
is a Good Samaritan mission.

WILL ROGERS

Parliament is the longest-running farce in the
West End.

CYRIL SMITH, MP

When the President does it, that means it's
not illegal.

RICHARD NIXON

Only people who look dull ever get into the
House of Commons, and only people who *are*
dull ever succeed there.

OSCAR WILDE

"

Don't get mad – get even.

ROBERT KENNEDY

Do unto others and do it fast.

ANON.

Do unto others and do it first.

DITTO

When your opponent is down, kick him.

DITTO

Vote early. Vote often.

CHICAGO (AND IRISH) ELECTION PROVERB

Politicians in both countries have one thing in common: they believe in approaching every question, topic or issue with an open mouth. They have one genuine dissimilarity: contrary to the docile British and the brash American image, in the House of Commons issues are pursued with the dexterity, style and subtlety of your average Millwall football supporter. By contrast, debates in the Senate and Congress are subdued, gentlemanly and dull – strange for a nation not noted for its modest approach to matters of public concern. In both countries (to misquote Harry Truman) Statesmen are politicians who've been dead for at least ten years.

BRITISH POLITICS

The most important thing to remember about twentieth century British politics is that Winston Churchill was descended from a Red Indian. Secondly, in Britain, unlike the fixed four-year term American system, we may have to wait up to *five* boring years for a General Election. In practice an election is nearly always called before the full term is completed, usually in order 'to dispel uncertainty among our allies', or 'to give the British people the earliest opportunity to approve plans for the second stage of our national recovery'. The true fact is that a government will try to call the election as soon after four years of office as it feels it can win. Calling an election in less than four years would create an impression of unseemly haste.

The major British parties have radically different manifestos, but on most points they all agree. Each stands for 'peace, freedom, the defence of Britain's traditional liberties, a return to full employment and justice for the most vulnerable members of society – the old, the sick and the disabled'. And what's more, they all promise to introduce 'measures to create lasting prosperity and improve the quality of life'. (For ease of reference, so do the Republicans and the Democrats.)

THE CONSERVATIVE (OR TORY) PARTY

The oldest of the British political parties and the party of Disraeli, Churchill, Macmillan and Mrs Thatcher. It's often said of Conservatives that they fight relentlessly to ensure that the rich get a square deal, while Disraeli remarked, 'A Conservative Government is an organized hypocrisy.'

Perhaps a fairer observation is that a Conservative is someone who is wholeheartedly committed to reform – but not yet. Or, to quote a left-wing Labour MP, 'They're a load of kippers: two-faced with no guts.'

Conservative policies are, broadly speaking (and please don't write in to contest this remark), Republican policies.

Conservatives are FOR:
>   Private enterprise
>   Law and order
>   NATO
>   Home ownership
>   Nuclear defence
>   The Common Market
>   Private education
>   Lower taxation
>   Privatization of public assets
>   Etc., etc.

Conservatives are AGAINST:
    State control
    Interventionism
    Devolution
    Public transport
    The abuse – or indeed use – of trade union power
    Public housing ('Council housing')
    Immigration

And remember:

> Conservatives are not necessarily stupid, but most stupid
> people are conservatives.
>
> JOHN STUART MILL

THE LABOUR PARTY

The Labour Party was founded in 1900 by the trade unions
and other socialist groups, and gained power for the first time
under Ramsay MacDonald in 1924. It's the party of Clement
Attlee, Hugh Gaitskell, Harold Wilson and, now, Glenys Kin-
nock. To quote George Orwell: 'As with the Christian religion,
the worst advertisement for Socialism is its adherents.'

Its first full-blooded Socialist programme was implemented
during the Government of 1945–51 when the National
Health Service was introduced and many industries nation-
alized. George Bernard Shaw once observed, 'We should have
had Socialism already but for the Socialists', and factionalism
in recent years has certainly affected the unity of the party
and its performance at the ballot box.

Former Conservative Prime Minister Ted Heath said, 'I seldom attack the Labour Party. They do it so well themselves.'
And indeed, this tendency led to the departure from the party
in recent years of several leading figures who subsequently
formed the more centrist Social Democratic Party.

The Labour Party is FOR:
>Nuclear disarmament
>Public enterprise
>Rail transport
>Council housing
>Increased public-sector investment
>The National Health Service
>A wealth tax
>Aid to developing countries
>The ethnic minorities
>Keynesianism

The Labour Party is AGAINST
>American nuclear bases in Britain
>The House of Lords
>Road transport
>Private education (except for Labour Cabinet Ministers)
>Private health care (ditto)
>Discrimination on the grounds of race, sex, class, merit, etc.

THE ALLIANCE

We know what happens to people who stay in the middle of the road. They get run over.

ANEURIN BEVAN

The Liberal Party recently formed an electoral alliance with the Social Democratic Party. While the SDP is but a few years old, the Liberal Party's history is buried in the mists of time. There are few Liberals still alive who can remember the time when their party was the natural opposition party to the Conservatives. The election of the first Labour Government in the 1920s marked the end of ninety years of alternating Liberal and Conservative supremacy. The Liberals are the party of Gladstone, Asquith, Lloyd George and, in more recent times, lots of people you won't have heard of. The present leader is David Steel.

They enjoy broad support from the electorate, but Britain's first-past-the-post electoral system ensures that the representation in Parliament of any party that gets less than a third of the votes is relatively tiny. An old joke guaranteed to inspire illiberal thoughts in the party concerns the arrival at the House of Commons of the Parliamentary Liberal Party in a taxi, and their meetings being held in a telephone box.

What the Alliance is most wholeheartedly FOR is, not unnaturally, electoral reform. Specifically this would mean replacing the existing electoral system with 'community proportional representation'. You don't want to know exactly how it works, but the outcome would be that the share of seats in Parliament would more accurately reflect a party's support among the voters. Or to put it another way, the current unrepresentative order would be replaced by a much more representative form of anarchy.

Additionally, Britain has had many other fascinating parties, all attracting their fair share of the vote, such as the Monster Raving Loony party; whatever Northern Ireland Protestant group is led by the Reverend Ian Paisley; and the British Nazi Party, otherwise known as the National Affront.

ELECTIONS

As the election approaches, each of the parties issues its manifesto. There's a limited number of titles for these publications and the parties take it in turns to use them. Three of the most popular are: *The Challenge of Our Times, Working Together for Britain,* and *The Road to Recovery.*

Each of the manifestos carries an introduction by the party leader. If the party leader is the Prime Minister and therefore leader of the party in power, the introduction will read:

Britain is once more a force to be reckoned with. It's true that formidable difficulties remain to be overcome, but after five years of our government national recovery has begun. When we came to office our country was suffering from both an economic crisis and a crisis of morale. This government created the conditions in which industry can prosper alongside a caring and responsible society. Together we have achieved much more over the past five years. We have laid the foundations for a dynamic and prosperous future. It is now right to ask for a new mandate to meet the challenge of our times.

If the party leader is in opposition, and wishes to take over the reins of government, the introduction will read like this:

In the last five years Britain has fared worse than any other major industrial country. When the present government took office they inherited falling unemployment and rising industrial growth. It was a legacy that was soon to be squandered. Our task in the next five years will be to restore our shattered national confidence and reverse Britain's industrial decline. We do not disguise the fact that putting Britain right will be an extremely difficult task. The economy must be patiently and steadily rebuilt. Our mission is to heal the wounds and rekindle among the British people a new sense of unity and common purpose.

Remember: terms like 'task', 'caring', 'unity', 'common purpose' and 'mandate' are not used in Britain by ordinary people going about their everyday lives, who are mostly bored by the whole exercise and especially with manifestos which, as Winston Churchill said, contain every cliché in the language except 'God is love' and 'Please adjust your dress before leaving.' Political manifestos are thus rather like car rental agreements. Nobody reads them.

THE HOUSE OF LORDS

The House of Lords is the upper house of the British Parliament. Membership is made up of hereditary peers, life peers, law lords, bishops and archbishops. There are more than 1,200 of them, of whom only about one-sixth attend regularly. Most of the others have never been seen or heard, and many may not actually exist. A young Labour backbencher recently described the House of Lords as 'a model of how to care for the elderly'. Those that do turn up have to be woken at regular intervals just to make sure they're still alive.

AMERICAN POLITICS: IS IT FOR REAL?

The World would not be in such a snarl
If Marx had been Groucho instead of Karl.
                              IRVING BERLIN

If you can fool some of the people all the time and all of the people some of the time, you've the makings of a good politician anywhere, but especially in America. There are two great political parties in the United States, Republican and Democrat. How do you tell them apart? Difficult for the amateur outsider, except by identifying them with individuals and their individual policies. Until 1828 (drop this lightly into the conversation) the Republican Party was an alternative name for the Democratic Party, until the advocates of high tariffs, led by John Quincy Adams, broke away and were called National Republicans or Whigs. The current Republicans were formed in 1854 from an alliance of National Republicans and Northern Democrats, both of which groups opposed the slave trade. The first Republican President was Abe Lincoln. Generally considered more right-wing than the Democrats (though watch simplistic comparisons), the GOP (Grand Old Party) uses the emblem of an elephant.

The Democrats originally opposed too much power for the Federal government when they were the Republican Party, if that's clear (see above). Andrew Jackson was arguably their first leader when the split came. Some of the modern party, especially in Massachusetts (but not the South) may with caution be considered just a fraction to the left of centre. The Democrats' motif is a donkey. So now you know.

Little or none of the above applies to New York City politics. As Christopher Morley said, 'New York is the Nation's thyroid gland,' and its uniqueness in so many ways is exemplified by it being cut off from the rest of the United States by a river. If Britain is an island and its inhabitants have peculiar qualities, Manhattan and its islanders have them all the more so, especially in politics. Just look at their mayor ... almost any of their mayors.

PRESIDENTIAL ELECTION CAMPAIGNS

> Where are you, Lee Harvey Oswald, now that your country really needs you?
>
> BOSTON GRAFFITI

Unlike a British election campaign (just three or four weeks of it if you're lucky), American Presidential campaigns last for three or even four years. Indeed, for simplicity's sake, many commentators will advise you to assume that they never stop. The hustings are always on screen, with primaries and conventions merely the late, late highlights of these non-stop, multi-ring circuses.

Primaries are state-by-state jockeyings for position through a mind-blowingly complex system, originally designed for a large country in an age when communications were determined by the pace of an average horse, of voting by registered members (delegates) of the parties (or by cabals of these parties). They may be of some interest on the east side of the Atlantic, simply because of the fascination of any political personality contest. But conventions are the finals of the Mr (could it be Ms?) United States of America Competition: 'And what are your interests?' 'What would you most like to achieve?' 'Who would you most like to emulate?' The vital statistics of the candidates are also declared: seventy-four (age), forty-two, thirty-eight, forty-two, and millions in the bank. Even Jimmy Carter managed to score a few debating points at his convention: 'When Ronald Reagan opens his mouth, you can hardly see his advisers' lips move.' The ceremony itself is the biggest thing since the word 'razzmatazz' was invented. Here is super-hype, mega-personality cultivation, mob hysteria, showbiz and politics not just walking hand in hand, but in the closest, sexiest, most intimate physical embrace. Blackpool was never like this.

Of course the action's not all allowed to happen front of stage; most of the real power play (and the activities of the Mafia seem mild by comparison) goes on in the convention hotel rooms and suites (the dressing rooms of power), where everything is sewn up nice and tidy before going public with the eventual unanimous choice of the party. Thus, the event in the convention hall is just the Westminster Abbey bit, the coronation scene. King-making is all done behind the bloodstained lattice-work. All the doors stay closed until the foul deed is done. The whole procedure verges on Lord Reith's ideal form of government: 'Despotism tempered by assassination'.

Above all, politics by photocall rules and the most mediagenic candidate wins in the end. In the morning-after words of Walter Mondale, 'I never warmed to television and it never warmed to me.' Perhaps he didn't follow Warren Harding's advice: 'I don't know much about Americanism, but it's a damn good word with which to carry an election.'

PRESIDENTS
AND PRIME MINISTERS

You will of course recall George Bernard Shaw's *The Applecart*, written around 1930. In it, the American Ambassador to the Court of St James calls on the British King Magnus, with the following interesting proposal: 'The Declaration of Independence is cancelled. The treaties that endorsed it are torn up. We have decided to rejoin the British Empire.'

He goes on to add, 'Perhaps I should have mentioned that one of our conditions will be that you will be Emperor. King may be good enough for this little island; but if we come in we shall require something grander.' And then he argues, 'We [Americans] are at home here ... we find here everything we are accustomed to: our industrial products, our books, our plays, our Christian Science churches, our osteopaths, our movies and talkies. ... A political union with us will be just the official recognition of already accomplished fact.

The King's Queen, Jemima, remarks: 'I think it a very good thing. We shall civilize these Americans. ... They know we are their natural superiors. You can see it by the way their women behave at court.'

Sadly, in the end the King turns the proposal down, perhaps recalling the fates of some American Emperor Presidents. On the basis that a little knowledge can be a very useful thing, glimpse if you will at some of those whose names and life stories will, if nothing else, provide you with the odd snippet for dinner-table conversation.

The ninth President, **William Henry Harrison**, was until Ronald Reagan the oldest man to be elected to the White House. By unfortunately dying after only thirty-one days in office, he holds an as yet unbeaten record. Not content with this, he also holds the record for the longest inaugural address. This lasted for one and three-quarter hours and provides a warning for others, since it probably precipitated his departure from this life, for it was delivered on a bitter winter day, so that he contracted fatal pneumonia. It was said that he was working on new tariff laws and may have overtaxed himself.

The eleventh President was, according to several eminent historians, one of America's finest, a fact that may astonish those who have never heard of James Knox Polk. By contrast, his successor **Zachary Taylor**, an experienced general but new to politics, goes down in history as the only President to have ridden his charger up the steps of the Capitol.

Good old **Franklin Pierce**, the fourteenth President, was known as a lightweight politician and a heavyweight drinker. He is best remembered as having been a classroom friend of Nathaniel Hawthorne. He at least could get rid of his hangovers in a hot bath; his predecessor **Millard Fillmore**, as all know, had a wife who insisted on having the first bathtub installed in the White House, around the year 1850.

To dedicated historians of trivia, President **James Buchanan**

is known as the only holder of this high office to have re-
mained unmarried throughout his life. To students of stronger
stuff, he is the man who let the country drift into the Civil
War. No one has ever argued that there was any connection
whatsoever between the two.

The twenty-ninth President was **Warren Gamaliel Harding**,
a man who, unlike Nixon, had the good sense to go and meet
his maker *before* the secrets of his private life and the corrupt
practices of some of his Cabinet led to impeachment. His successor, **Calvin** 'Silent Cal' **Coolidge**, who was said to be more
famous for his silences than his speeches, elevated inactivity
into a political philosophy. He did however coin the phrase,
'The business of America is business.' It is also said that
Coolidge's significance lies in his having been the most ridi-
culed President before Ford. To Mencken, 'Coolidge's chief
feat was to sleep more than any other President.' If we are to
believe the latest reports, there is currently another candidate
in the running for that title.

To return to **Gerald Ford**, he became Vice-President when
Agnew admitted fraud, and the President when Nixon did,
without having to fight a single election, a truly remarkable
feat. (Spiro Agnew has been described as the only politician
in America with real convictions.) The Ford presidency was
one that brought a bit of humour and buffoonery back into
political life after the boring Watergate years. As the *Guardian*
said in 1974, 'A year ago Gerald Ford was unknown
throughout America. Now he's unknown throughout the
world.' Still, **Ronald Reagan**, the Errol Flynn of the B
movies, is still the only President to have shared a bed with
a chimpanzee called Bonzo. He will also be remembered
for having done for jelly beans what **Jimmy Carter** did for
peanuts.

In comparison with such a distinguished list, British Prime
Ministers provide even the most dedicated with little to laugh
about.

Rivalling each other as the man to hold the shortest term

of office are the household names of the Duke of Wellington, who was Prime Minister for twenty-two days, and of course our old friend The Right Honourable Sir James Waldegrave, Knight of the Garter who, as every schoolboy knows, held office for five days in June 1757.

Britain has a long way to go to beat America in another field. Poor Spencer Perceval is the only Prime Minister to have been assassinated, which happened on 11 May 1812 when by chance he ran into a crazed man, one of many to be found, day or night, in the House of Commons. Shot in the chest, he died before a doctor could be found.

William Ewart Gladstone may be best remembered for his missionary work among the fallen women of London. These ladies of the night called him 'Old Gladeye'. He also (nudge, nudge; wink, wink) kept whips in his cellar.

Lord Rosebery was the only Prime Minister we can find who both owned a Derby winner and married a Rothschild, prompting Claud Cockburn to comment that Rosebery 'demonstrated that it was possible to improve one's financial status and run the Empire without neglecting the study of form'.

Andrew Bonar Law is widely known as Britain's most unknown modern Prime Minister. Asquith is said to have remarked at Bonar Law's funeral: 'It is fitting that we should have buried the Unknown Prime Minister by the side of the Unknown Soldier.' Of himself Law said: 'There go my people. I must follow them. I am their leader.'

Neville Chamberlain is best known for his umbrella and his trip to get Hitler's autograph.

Sir Alec Douglas-Home is the only Prime Minister to have played first-class cricket (Middlesex in 1924/25) and to have guided the Treasury's financial policy with the aid of matchsticks.

Edward Heath was the first bachelor to become Prime Minister since Pitt in 1784, and is best remembered for his efforts to give the working people of Britain more leisure time – with a bold but unappreciated move to introduce a three-day working week to allow more people to enjoy organ music and ocean racing.

James Callaghan was Britain's last Labour Prime Minister.

7
Class, Status and Rank

"

The English never smash in a face. They merely refrain from asking it to dinner.

MARGARET HALSEY

... the Cabots speak only to Lowells
And the Lowells speak only to God.

TRAD.

I'd expect to be robbed in Chicago
But not in the land of the cod,
So I hope that the Cabots and Lowells
Will mention the matter to God.

OGDEN NASH
(On having his car broken into in Boston)

Actually I vote Labour, but my butler is a Tory.

ATTRIBUTED TO LORD MOUNTBATTEN

You simply cannot hang a millionaire in America.

BOURKE COCKRAN

"

This section is about class and how to outclass. For example, if Americans come the superior and talk about poor old threadbare toothless bulldogs who have lost an Empire, etc., etc., and isn't it cute that England is smaller than New England, your stalwart Brit can always take them by the metaphorical lapels and drawl: 'Look, Wilmer (you are all called Wilmer, aren't you?) just remember that the Sahara Desert is the same size as America and twice as cultural.'

Or, again: 'OK, so you have ten thousand golf courses, no clocks in your Vegas casinos, and camel hunting is illegal in Arizona – that makes you special . . . ?' Couple that with, 'Face facts, Wilmer – your bald-headed eagles ain't even bald.' This sort of thing goes down a treat. Try it, provided you're bigger than him.

CLASS IN BRITAIN

Rather than outclassing, let us address ourselves to serious problems such as whether there is a class problem (war) in Britain. Matthew Arnold divided the British into three classes: philistines, barbarians and populace. You will always find a few (usually of the extreme left and frequently themselves scions of upper or middle class families – these are, or used to be, known as ivory-tower socialists) who argue the class war case. Facts are that there is a great deal of upward social mobility, and a fair share of the reverse process, including a good (and much publicized) smattering of the titled aristocracy who are currently bus conductors, window cleaners or policemen. Indeed, many are parking-lot attendants cum tourist guides, for there is a growing number of landed gentry (i.e., inheritors of large tracts of family land) who increasingly open their stately houses to the *hoi polloi* (masses) on a charge basis in order to pay off death duties (inheritance taxes) or the rates (local taxes). Others think of the upper crust as just a few crumbs sticking together.

For centuries British society has been divided, not just by
Arnold, but also by conventional wisdom, into three classes:
the UPPER, landed class which, by birth, social standing, ed-
ucation and wealth has been in a position to grind the
WORKING class into an early grave in the dark satanic mills,
factories, coal mines, and the pigsties of the peasantry, all in
support of capitalism and the profit motive. To quote Michael
Foot, 'There was never a more bloody-minded set of thugs
than the British ruling class.' In between these two classes
was crushed the pliant MIDDLE class, which was worthy,
churchgoing, professional, industrious and very boring. At
the top of the middle and the bottom of the upper classes
there was a grey area through which people occasionally rose
and sank, and doubtless the same was true between the
bottom of the middle and the top of the working, though
nobody cared much about that.

Then, in the first decade of the second half of this present
century, certain wise sociologists and linguists and subsequently lickspittle journalists who fed upon them, decided
that they would extrapolate from the thinking of Benjamin
Disraeli (yes, the same one), who said in his book, *Sybil*, 'I
was told that the privileged and the people formed two nations.' These great thinkers said that there were, if not two
nations, two classes, divided by their speech patterns and
vowel sounds, namely the fashionable U (for upper) and the
unfashionable Non-U. (These terms were introduced to the
language in a book edited by Nancy Mitford.)

Despite the dedicated efforts of recent governments to drag
Mr Disraeli's two nations into being (in simplistic terms they
have succeeded across large stretches of the country, as wit-
ness the unemployment figures) when one looks long and
hard at the situation, there are, in fact, four distinct classes
in this country, the traditional upper, middle and lower
classes, and the 'NEW CLASS'.

As to locating the 'new class', in a formal dinner-party
placement it overlaps the lower half of the upper and the top
echelon of the middle, eschewing that strange breed of gold-

chain wearers known sometimes as the scampi-belt class. In less formal circumstances, it prevails over all competition (except Royal). It is that trans-class group of socially mobile achievers, often quite considerably influenced by things and styles American, who actually run the country (and quite a few other countries besides), despite the fact that members of some of the traditional classes, particularly the upper class, think that *they* still do so.

The 'new class' has two categories of member, like the best London clubs, temporary or probationary members and life members. The Archbishop of Canterbury, Norman Tebbit, Paul McCartney and Sebastian Coe are life members; the Bishop of Durham, John Selwyn Gummer, Boy George and Zola Budd are still completing their probation. (Zola comes up for full membership at the next meeting, delayed only by a check on her residential qaulification.) Probationary members either get promoted or remain temporary members for a month, a year, a decade, and then pass into semi-obscurity, either moving over to emulate members of the upper class with a house in Gloucestershire or at least the stockbroker belt, or falling on hard times and ending up in Ealing or even the North of England as clones of the middle class. Or worse.

Members of the 'new class' will be well educated, by no means necessarily at a public (private) school, by no means necessarily at Oxbridge, but still preferably at both. Money earned is not an absolute criterion of membership but, like Oxbridge, it helps. Accents should be not too ethnic or regional, though some types of Welsh, Scots and West Country accents are all right in moderation. (A slight Irish lilt is considered an advantage in some callings.) A Birmingham accent remains a decided handicap, as does a Geordie (north-eastern) accent, though the latter is mainly on the grounds of incomprehensibility.

Style is important and thus Babycham, VP sherry or lager and lime, or pastimes like bingo, ballroom dancing or goldfish keeping are unlikely to feature heavily.

Members of the 'new class' would love their memberships to be hereditary, but they know that at best they are only life peers in the national order of merit – dukes like Duke Ellington rather than the Duke of Kent, barons only of industry, no longer lording it over the peasants but just over society columnists such as Nigel Dempster and William Hickey (if they are lucky).

CLASS IN AMERICA

Frances Trollope, Anthony's mother, said it all in a highly unpopular book on America that she wrote in the 1830s, where she talked about 'the fable of equality'. John Adams, the second President of the new United States, believed that

'People of all nations are naturally divided into two sorts, the gentlemen and the simplemen.' The gentlemen are generally those who are rich, live in houses 'that you can't see from the road' and are descended from families in public life. It has been said that it takes three generations plus one good guess on the stock market to produce an American gentleman. What rises quickly can sink just as fast. Andrew Carnegie once remarked that you could go 'from shirtsleeves to shirt-sleeves' in three generations. 'Inequality is as dear to the American heart as liberty itself,' wrote William Dean Howells: 'all men may be born equal but most of us spend the better part of our born days in trying to be as unequal as we can.'

The Old Guard, the self-appointed American aristocracy (none of them called Wilmer) are descended from the first arrivals. Being English-speaking, they were already one jump ahead – except for the Irish, who opted out of the robber baron race, and became cops; some would say they made the best choice. As we would expect from America, money and power counted even in those rarefied strata. The proud FFVs, the First Families of Virginia, were not the first on the scene but the first to *make it*. Rivalry between groups of colonial descendants is keen. The formidable DAR, the Daughters of the American Revolution, who democratically take their numbers from succeeding generations of offspring of other ranks who served in the revolutionary armies, have less cachet than the Society of Colonial Dames, who select from officers only. Even grander are the direct male descendants of officers, who form the Society of the Cincinnati. More exclusive still is the Order of the Founders and Patriots, whose ancestors were living in the colonies prior to 1700 and fought in Washington's army. The Philadelphia branch of the Society of Colonial wars makes it even more difficult by limiting its membership to two hundred worthies. You do have to be born into the Old Guard, but although they may form the backbone of it, they are only a part of American 'society'.

The *Social Register*, the 'black book' which in its heyday published its list of the socially acceptable in twenty-one American cities, now gives the names, addresses (summer and winter) and telephone numbers of the *crème de la crème* in a meagre dozen. It was started in 1887 as a business venture by one Louis Keller of Summit, New Jersey (he also owned a golf club, a dairy and a tinpot railroad). Boston, Baltimore and Philadelphia, feeling superior, hint that you can *buy* your way into the New York book. No one really knows how you get in. You can be removed for misbehaving, divorcing or marrying the wrong person. Washington's *Green Book* mixes shakers and movers with the socially prominent. The great American Jewish families, excluded from the *Social Register*, the 'Jewish Grand Dukes' – the Strausses, Warburgs, Lehmans, Schiffs, Loebs, Ochses, Sulzburgers, *et al.* – kept themselves to themselves, intermarrying and avoiding publicity until the middle of this century.

An idea fundamental to Americans is that the right behaviour is the key to success. Behaviour can be modified. You may have been a poor hick but you don't have to stay that way. Hope springs eternal in the American breast. The bestseller list is awash with self-help books. You *can* make it to the top. Americans admire and reward enterprise, but you have to play by the rules once you get there. (Incidentally, if you're kidnapped, any ransom paid is tax-deductible.) If you don't look, sound, eat and decorate your house in a certain way, no one will *know* you've made it.

The symbols, trappings and outward show of success (money and power) have to be exclusive. If everyone could afford to play polo, it wouldn't be the same, now would it? Paddle tennis is the status sport at the moment, because there are no *public* courts.

Speech is not the minefield in America it is in Britain. Bad grammar is tolerated to a generous extent, and regional accents don't matter. There is no received *American*. Once you have made it to the top it is correct to relax. Your clothing (the best) can have the initials on the inside. Use the family Louis Vuitton luggage (anything too large to carry can be used as furniture) *only* if it is old and battered. But remember that the Old Guard recognize each other – rich or poor. They have what most Americans lack, a common background. America is too big and Americans too mobile for people who have known each other all their lives to stick together. It is much easier for the old boy network to function in a country the size of Britain. The exception to this is the Mafia, but if you're not of Sicilian blood, forget it: they don't accept converts.

8
Lifestyles

"

An Englishman thinks he is moral when he is only uncomfortable.

GEORGE BERNARD SHAW

The terrible newly-imported American doctrine that everyone ought to do something.

SIR OSBERT SITWELL

It is an American characteristic not to stop running even after you have arrived.

CLIVE JAMES

We are a nation that has always gone in for the loud laugh, the wow, the belly laugh, and the dozen other labels for the roll-'em-in-the-aisles gagerissimo.

JAMES THURBER

"

ODD BRITISH WAYS

An Englishman, even if he is alone, forms an orderly queue of one.

GEORGE MIKES

Every foreigner knows what comes top of the list under this heading. The British love queueing. They will appear to queue for anything, given half a chance, and have been known to join a queue and then ask the reason for it. In Britain, one person waiting for anything is automatically a queue, and consequently queue-jumping comes only slightly behind mass murder and treason in the national morality stakes. The American equivalent would be lighting a cigarette in an elevator.

Secondly, they, or rather their media, are fascinated to the point of tedium about industrial relations. There is nothing they like better than a good strike with lots of heavy picketing. Then the (largely) right-wing press go heavy on finding reds under every bed, or at least gathered around braziers at the gates of the blacked factories. They have developed a whole jargon ('flying pickets' are ones who move from site to site) and for weeks on end, front pages and editorials are full of stories, particularly if any individual union (labor) leader can be identified as some form of neo-commie extremist. In the States, similar events, such as a miners' strike, would be relegated to the foot of page three of the *Wall Street Journal*. Another British preoccupation (again particularly in the media) is a love of disasters – plane, train and bus crashes command particular pre-eminence over any item of world news.

Other British deviations include spending too much time talking, writing and reading about, as well as viewing on television, soap operas like *Coronation Street* (which the tabloids give as much coverage to as they do to the Royal Family or even *Dallas*), the weather, cricket, snooker, Arthur Scargill, football hooligans and anything to do with sex or violence.

The masses have a healthy disregard for politics (party political broadcasts on television offer an occasion to brew up a
cup of tea, have another beer or walk the dog), alternating
bouts of disinterest with periods of extreme indifference.

Additionally, Americans may find the following other things
about the British just a fraction puzzling.

WHY do they put ferrets down their trousers?

WHY do adults still keep their soft toys?

WHY do they think men in drag are so funny? (And is the
old British stereotype of the bowler-hatted, furled umbrella-
carrying city gent being replaced by Boy George clones?)

WHY do they give you a limp two-fingered handshake? Is it
only the upper orders? (Americans are taught that a firm,
bone-crunching grip indicates strength of character.)

WHY do they pronounce 'Cholmondeley' as 'Chumley' and
'Leveson-Gower' as 'Lewson-Gore'?

WHY do they apologize if *you* tread on *their* toes?

WHY do they wrap their beloved fish and chips in filthy old
newspapers?

WHY don't they like English heavy metal groups as much as
Americans do?

WHY they don't get their pre-ordered interval drinks stolen
in theatres?

WHY do they watch sheepdog trials on television?

WHY are British political scandals about sex, while American
ones are about money or criminal deeds?

WHY, if the Earl of Sandwich invented them, can't they make
a decent one?

Fish and Chips

One particular British fetish which will be noted by most American visitors is the British attitude to animals. As Alice Thomas Ellis wrote,

> The totem of the English was a small animal – furry, stuffed and articulate. Winnie the Pooh vied with the Queen (God trailing in the distance) for the forefront of the mind of the English middle class. ... Did any other people – apart from Red Indians – make such a fuss of creatures which in reality they were in the habit of chasing, shooting, poisoning, trapping or beating to death with sticks?

The British have no answer to this, but solve their dilemma by subscribing vastly greater sums to the RSPCA (Royal Society for the Prevention of Cruelty to Animals) than to the NSPCC (National Society for the Prevention of Cruelty to Children – not Royal, you will note). And the Animal Liberation Front at times seems to put the IRA into the shade when it starts poisoning the nation's most beloved chocolate bars.

One last fetish: the British keep a stiff upper lip but seem to Americans to complain in private – a low, ineffectual mutter of whingeing and blingeing. They don't nag the creep in the queue at the supermarket who has more than eight items in the express line, but purse their lips and roll their eyes silently. Americans not only speak up but write to manufacturers of faulty goods, legislate on things like food and cosmetic labelling (health conscious) and, if they don't like them, take things back to shops.

It is all summed up in the traditonal American tale about how you can tell which aeroplane is British Airways: it's the one that whines after the engines have stopped.

A FEW THINGS ABOUT THE AMERICANS THAT PUZZLE THE BRITISH

WHY do they find our accent so funny? (Or, if not, are actually impressed by it?)

WHY do they find Benny Hill so funny?

WHY do the drains steam in New York City, and the garbage and post boxes look so much alike?

WHY, with such huge automobiles, do they acquiesce to a speed limit of 55 mph – and even abide by it?

WHY, if New York is really a twenty-four-hour-a-day mecca of capitalism, is it impossible to pay by, or cash, a personal cheque?

WHY do most New York cab drivers not speak English, and the ones that do still have this thing about Mayor Lindsay?

WHY does an American sandwich always arrive with salad and french fries?

WHY do they have cockroaches even on the thirtieth floor of a luxury skyscraper?

WHY do they go to shrinks even more than the British actually think they do?

WHY, with ethnic roots stretching back to almost every country in the world, does the 'abroad doesn't matter' argument in the last resort win the most popular votes?

LIFESTYLES

A guide to lifestyles in both countries is nowhere better illustrated than by looking at:

CONTRASTING FEMINIST PREOCCUPATIONS

United States	Great Britain
Two-career couples	Single-parent families
Gloria Steinem's apparently more moderate stance	Germaine Greer's apparently more moderate stance

Child-care options

Post-feminist heterosexual lust

Career choices

Tax breaks for child care

Pregnant executive wear

Self-defence aerosol weapons

Stand-up comedy workshops

Public speaking workshops

Commuter marriages

'The Gender Gap'

The ERA

The National Women's Political Caucus

Marriage as a socio-economic arrangement

Role-sharing

Parenting

Relocation assistance for spouses

Becoming computerate

Crêche facilities

Feminist separatism

Unwaged consciousness-raising

Female circumcision

Sexual harassment at the office

Self-defence workshops

Street theatre

Keening

'Self-definition'

Black feminist workshops

Feminist collectives

Consciousness-raising groups

Traditional patriarchal institutions

Combating heterosexism

Lesbian motherhood

Domestic violence

Women-only no-smoking discos

AMERICAN IDEAS WHICH THE BRITISH TRIED TO RESIST AND FAILED

The Price is Right

Late-night supermarkets (though they resist a bit by making the aisles too narrow)

Sunday paper comics

The People's Court

McDonald's Chicken McNuggets – just don't stop to won-

der what part of the chicken *are* the McNuggets.
Burger King, etc. (though they still try for non-conformity by attempting to discuss the menu when they reach the head of the queue)

THINGS THAT WORRY AMERICANS BUT DON'T WORRY THE BRITISH – YET

Minority groups with special problems: the children of the super-rich
Sexual casualty: the abandoned male
Plastic surgery: rebuilding the cocaine-abused nose
Etiquette: addressing a gay couple
Children: transcontinental divorced parents
Sexual abuse: male rape
Prejudice: speciesism
Divorce problems: The working dad
Entertainers: black country and western singers
Therapy problem: falling in love with your sexual surrogate

WHAT MOTORISTS LOOK FOR IN A CAR

In Great Britain:
  Price

In the United States:
  Fuel efficiency
  Rear deck lid spoilers
  Long-range radar detectors
  Accent stripes
  Anti-sway bars
  Five-year anti-corrosion warranties
  Cruise control
  Multi-adjustable drivers' seats
  Mobile security systems
  Multi-port fuel injection
  Onboard automotive computers
  Engine management systems
  'Aggressive low-end torque'
  Fade-resistant brakes
  Optimal predictability tyres
  and quartz synthesised cassette tuners and angled horn
    tweeter speaker systems

While we are on the subject of lifestyles, let us take a brief look at the bewildering world of:

CRICKET*

Jokes about explaining cricket to foreigners (which, because it is basically an English game, means explaining it to the Scots, Irish and Welsh as well) are legion. The basic one goes something like this: You have two sides, one is out in the field and one is in. Each man on the side that's in goes out

*By Michael Shea.

and when he's out he goes in and the next man goes in until he's out. When they are all out, the side that's been out in the field goes in and the side that's been in goes out and tries to get those who are in, out. Sometimes you get men still in and not out, etc. etc.

There are one-day games, three-day games and five-day games. The five-day games are played between various members of the Commonwealth (ex-British Commonwealth, ex-ex-British Empire) who for some reason like and play the game. These five-day games are known as Test Matches. Cricket is a four-innings game as compared to baseball's nine innings. Each innings consists of each of eleven players on a side having a turn to bat. The team that wins is the one that gets more runs between a set of two wickets (three vertical sticks with two little ones balanced across the top), the total being that when each has got the other team out twice.

For the luckless spectator, help is often at hand thanks to the British weather, which frequently causes the game to be rained off. Believe it or not, even at the end of a five-day game, it is common for the result to be a draw. But then many people think of cricket as a habit rather than a sport, so nobody worries very much. I hope that's all clear.

Co-Author's dissent: Mr Frost would like to apologize to cricket-lovers for the palpable unfairness of Mr Shea's outpourings above. They prove once again, alas, that there are certain finer elements of English life that the Scots are still incapable of appreciating. However, the battle goes on.

Co-Author's re-dissent: Mr Shea would like to note that if cricket is one of the 'finer elements' of English life, that makes a devastating point about England. He rests his case.

Final Co-Author's dissent: Mr Frost feels that Mr Shea is wise to rest his case. It was beginning to look extremely tired.

9
Food and Drink

"

If the British can survive their meals, they can survive anything.

GEORGE BERNARD SHAW

More and more in American restaurants advertising has taken over the menu. You're sold on the meal before you have even started.

CECIL BEATON

If American men are obsessed with money, American women are obsessed with weight. The men talk of gain and the women talk of loss and I do not know which talk is the more boring.

MARYA MANNES

Alcohol and nicotine
Wipe half the world from the scene.
Lack of both – it's safe to say,
Take the rest at close of play.

MICHAEL SINCLAIR

"

BRITISH EATING HABITS

The most important thing you will notice when you observe your Standard Brit is that while eating he or she performs the intricately absurd exercise of holding the knife in the right hand and pushing the food (difficult without practice) on to the curved back of the fork, which is held in the left hand. If you're reading this on a flight, you'll find it even more difficult using the little plastic implements with which you are provided.

'Cuisine' and 'British' (like 'American' and 'Culture') used to be contradictions in terms. There was an old adage (maybe we invented it) about visitors and tourists enjoying Britain so long as they brought their own sandwiches. Feeding standards and culinary expertise were not parts of the Great British Tradition. (There were also the other cranks, like the famous British politician who always took food with him and was once found cooking sausages over a primus stove in his Paris hotel room).

It has all changed fundamentally and radically. Now only a fool eats badly, not only in London, but in quite a few other places in Britain as well – though it is always better to be prepared.

BRITISH FOOD & DRINK TO LOOK OUT FOR (IN BOTH SENSES OF THE WORD)

Beer Flatter, darker and warmer than any transatlantic drink. Draught beer is categorized, in England, as mild or bitter, and in Scotland as light or heavy. You'll have to experiment at length in order to discover why. (Such are the demands of research.)

Bubble and squeak This concoction is a combination of mashed potatoes and cabbage. Yes, really. For purists these must be left-overs. They are mixed together and fried until brown. Well worth a detour – in order to miss. (As a close substitute, try any meal in a motorway service area.)

Chips French fries. Served with everything, especially north of Watford. Try the Bradford speciality: vindaloo and chips.

Cock-a-leekie soup Chicken stewed in prunes and leeks. Not much better than bubble and squeak.

Coffee Don't complain. You too may be old and weak yourself one day. In the words of Fred Allen, 'English coffee tastes like water squeezed out of a wet sleeve.'

Faggots These are pig left-overs made into a form of sausage. Good for jokes, bad for the digestion. (Note the Huddersfield term of endearment: 'You old faggot.')

Finnan haddie   The first edible dish on our list so far. A kind of smoked haddock heated and eaten with butter, usually for breakfast.

Kedgeree   A relic of empire. It's smoked haddock cooked with rice and chopped hard-boiled eggs, often flavoured with curry powder. First cooked for the British in India during the nineteenth century, and hasn't changed much since.

Marmite   Marmite is a curious British invention made from yeast and vegetable extract. If you arrive in Hollywood and make it known that you are carrying some jars of Marmite with you, the entire English colony will be at your door. Its habit-forming qualities suggest that it may be an as-yet un-detected drug.

Mulligatawny soup   This is a beef soup flavoured with curry, discovered by English cooks in between their experiments to invent kedgeree. Relatively acceptable.

Scotch egg   A rubbery hard-boiled egg that has been encased in a coffin of sausage meat and breadcrumbs, then deep fried. You're right: appalling.

Shepherd's pie   Left-over lamb (or almost anything) dis-guised with Worcester or even soy sauce, covered with mashed potatoes and then browned to the correct degree. Good for anorexics.

Shorts (short drinks)   Expect them very very short and ice-free.

Spotted dick   A steamed pudding with raisins. Its main vir-tue is conversational (cf. 'Faggots').

Tea   Notably transport caff style – thick as axle grease.

Toad in the hole   English sausages baked in Yorkshire pud-ding.

Tripe   Served with onions as England's answer to the Arab's sheep's eye.

Yorkshire pudding What you combine with sausages in order to make Toad in the hole.

THE BRITISH BREAKFAST

The British breakfast is the meal that Somerset Maugham advised all visiting gastronomes to partake of three times a day while visiting the UK. It was reliable, plentiful and more difficult to spoil in the cooking. As a piece of advice this is a trifle wild, but he had a point. Breakfast is, at best, a silent meal, a time for introspection, a time for nursing hangovers, and not for chatter. There are still some officers' messes in the Army where the individual who wears his cap at table is indicating that he does not wish to be spoken to. Not a bad custom.

Hotel and restaurant menus have two types of breakfast: 'Continental' and 'full'. The former is your very basic tea or coffee, juice and toast or rolls with butter and orange marmalade. (No real Brit will take jam, i.e. spreads made from fruits other than oranges, for breakfast, though honey or Marmite (see above) are permitted.)

The full British breakfast (sadly on the decline) is cooked and, after cereals, cornflakes, etc., will comprise at its best, fried eggs, sausages, bacon, mushroom, tomatoes or, as a sideline, kippers (smoked herring) and kedgeree. In Scotland porridge (oatmeal) *must* be eaten only with salt. There is a prize somewhere for the first visitor to be offered fresh orange juice with breakfast in any British catering establishment outside London. (Any American asking, 'Is this orange juice fresh?' will be assured that the can has only just been opened.)

AMERICAN EATING AND DRINKING HABITS

American food in general is sweeter, including the bread, and they have strange things like jello salad, and cook with strange herbs, marshmallows and brown sugar – a sweet tooth, albeit in fear of cavities.

Beyond being aware that there are more nutrients in the cornflake packaging than there is in a bowl of regular corn-flakes, the first thing that the British visitor will also note about American eating habits, involves the handling of cut-lery. All non-left-handed Americans hold their forks in their right hands while eating in order to, as it were, spoon food into their mouths, just like any well-brought-up Brit was trained *not* to do by nanny at nursery teas.

A lot of nonsense is spoken in Britain about American junk food, though it hasn't stopped it being one of America's grea-test exports after *Dallas*. Until recently, the British thought of American cuisine as always coming in clingfilm wrapping and mainly consisting of hamburgers, popcorn and coke. Hard drinks were all cocktails dressed up in very strange disguises. Ignore most of what you think you know. Ameri-cans are now and have long been much more diet- and health-conscious than the British and, consequently, even fast food establishments tend to dish up meals that are not only tasty but also relatively wholesome.

Otherwise the British visitor should do what the American visitor does if he wants a good meal in the UK, and try for ethnicity. While there are plenty of *haute cuisine* and specialty restaurants, steakhouses and seafood especially, go Greek, Japanese, Vietnamese or indeed Cambodian. Coffee shops offer a range of meals, not just coffee, and are excellent for break-fasts (see below) or if you have the challenge of travelling with small children. And when out on the town on a pub crawl, always remember that piece of Harvard medical graf-fiti: 'Never accept a drink from a urologist.'

DRINKS

Beer   'Those who drink beer will think beer.' (Washington Irving) Therefore expect it gassy and light.

Biscuits   Ask for cookies. (NB. Nobody says, 'That's the way the cookie crumbles' any more.)

Coffee   Usually reasonable and plentiful, though there are dangers even in America: 'If this is coffee, bring me tea. If it's tea, bring me coffee.' (Abraham Lincoln)

Drink laws   Vary very much from state to state. In some counties that are quasi-dry, try bootlegging.

Iced tea   Will help you recover from your pre-lunch martinis.

Shorts   Long and ice-packed.

Whisky   Ask for Scotch, otherwise you'll get bourbon, which isn't bad if you're in the right frame of mind, as in: 'Everybody should believe in something: I believe I'll have another drink.'

THE AMERICAN BREAKFAST

You can, by and large, get the same or almost the same as the great British breakfast, though you have to learn some of the jargon. For example, you may wish your fried eggs turned, in which case it's 'easy over' (or 'sunny side down') as opposed to 'sunny side up'. Try also French toast (egg dipped), hash browns (potato) and flapjacks. But you may need to adjust your palate to some of the sweeter breakfast tastes such as pancakes thick with cream and honey or the ubiquitous 'Danish' pastries (prune-stuffed ones are a common but daunting delight), which generally need plentiful supplies of coffee to wash them down. American bacon is always sliced very thin and therefore (particularly if perchance you are actually cooking it after a long night astray in unfamiliar surroundings) will shrivel to a crisp tenth of its original size if you take your eyes off it for a moment. Best eaten in a BLT – i.e., Bacon, Lettuce and Tomato Sandwich.

Beware, oh ye who like your food straight and simple. Even the best-cooked bacon, sausage and eggs will be served up surrounded and garnished with an amazing choice of fruits, pineapple or watermelon bites, cherries or even strawberries. The same applies to many American dishes, where over-fussy presentation may be most off-putting. Sweet and savoury mixed is not just confined to cranberry sauce with the turkey: you may reel from the sight of a decent bacon sandwich doused, apparently Western-style, with a liberal coating of maple syrup and cream.

A final word on American eating habits: the further west you go, the more you will come upon the strange habit of mixing meat and fish: filet mignon with lobster tails (called 'Surf and Turf', 'Sea and Ski' etc.), or T-bone and king prawns. When you get into that sort of frontier environment, your sense of reality tends to diminish, and such things are decidedly less unthinkable than you may think from 6,000 miles away.

AMERICAN FOOD & DRINK TO LOOK OUT FOR (IN BOTH SENSES OF THE WORD)

Acorn squash   A delicious yellow squash found in New England, cut in half, and baked with lots of butter and honey in the middle. Crisp under the grill just before devouring.

Apple knocker   During cold winters in Minnesota, manly natives drink a combination of 1 ounce vodka, 4 ounces hot cider, some nutmeg, a piece of lemon and a cinnamon stick. Not recommended for drivers on the interstate freeway.

Big Weenie   A mile-long hot dog. Too much of a dubiously good thing. (Also popular as an anatomical description.)

Blondie   Like a brownie, which is a fudge cake square, only this is without chocolate dough and with chocolate chips. Calorie count about as disastrous as Acorn squash.

Boilermaker   Shot of whiskey dropped in a stein of beer. A major pick-me-up and put-me-down.

Coney Island (or Coney dog)   A special version of the hot dog. Covered with chili and chopped onions, it tastes a lot better than it smells (and the taste is none too good).

Haagen-Dazs Swiss Almond Vanilla ice cream   This has a pronounced almond flavour *and* a pronounced vanilla flavour, plus a pronounced Haagen-Dazs. The authors, fortunately, don't have to pronounce it – that's for you to do, if you want some. We only have to spell it. But if you can twist your tongue around the name, your tastebuds will soon get their reward.

Healthburgers   In our view, the most sensible way to follow a vegetarian diet is to let the cow do it and then take one's own in roast beef and hamburger. This, however, is not the sort of argument designed to appeal to the type of person who eats healthburgers. Anyway, they are there if you want them.

Hush puppies   Cute little round fried cornmeal balls. Served in Southern restaurants, usually on a plate with about nineteen other fried dishes.

Monte Cristo   Three layers of egg-dipped French toast with ham and cheese between the layers, covered in soft sugar and maple syrup. Served hot. Quite irresistible.

Plantation deep dish apple crunch   Sort of an apple pie without the crust. Not to be confused with Apple Knocker or Apple Brown Betty.

Reuben sandwich   Because of its bulk (it's made of hot corned beef and cheese) one recent British gastronome, hypnotized perhaps by its rich, plump succulence, can be excused for calling it a Rubens sandwich.

Root beer   Tastes as good as it sounds. Imagine a large glass of cough mixture with ice.

Sociable garlic dip   You get the taste but your friends don't get the smell. That's the theory, anyway. Warm ice cream would be an equivalent. Or cold mashed potato. Warm ice cream *added* to cold mashed potato would have the same consistency as sociable garlic dip but would, in fact, be tastier.

Tofutti   A non-dairy 'ice cream' made from soybean curd, which is low in calories, cholesterol-free, sold two million gallons in 1984 and leaves us as it comes to us: cold.

RELIEF FACILITIES

Which way to the euphemism?

DINNER GUEST TO HOSTESS

For the unwary the continuing fashion for euphemisms can be fraught with danger, particularly when applied, as it is increasingly, to lavatories. Avoid at all costs, the use of the word 'toilet' since, from the days of Nancy Mitford, it is such a dangerously Non-U word in British circles. (Indeed couples have been known to be expelled from smart dinner parties just for intimating that they desire to use such a down-market establishment.) Use the word 'loo' cautiously, especially in Cornwall where it is so easily confused with Looe, a picturesque tourist attraction whose residents do not appreciate their historic streets being used for such unpicturesque purposes. It is incomprehensible in most of the States. (The derivation of 'loo' from *L'eau* is certainly wrong. For some time during the sixteenth and seventeenth centuries, a lavatory was known in France as a *lieu à l'anglaise*, thanks to Sir John Harrington, inventor of the flushing mechanism.)

In this fundamentally important area, in both Britain and America, there has been a hasty and ill-advised tendency to adopt mealy-mouthed wording and, even worse, diagrams and illustrations on the doors of such places. Instead of the brusque, straightforward, informative quality of 'Ladies' and 'Gentlemen' or even 'Men' and 'Women' there has been a flood – correction, a rash – correction, a plethora – of cutesie titles.

In the UK the advent of the Common Market has had a decided influence: 'Senores y Senoritas', 'Mesdames et Messieurs' and 'Damen und Herren' are the order of the day. Visitors to Scotland should be particularly warned of the experience of one American visitor who spent fifty-three minutes trying to assess the relative prevailing strengths of Scottish dialect and Scottish spelling before deciding whether to enter a small, square building marked 'Laddies'.

In America, ethnic and Wild West influences tend to abound:

> Guys and Dolls
> Hombres and Chiquitas
> Braves and Squaws
> Critters and Cuties
> Gangsters and Molls
> Cats and Mice
> Priests and Nuns
> GI Joes and GI Joans

David Frost recalls his English secretary returning embarrassedly to a dinner party of twelve in Dallas to ask, 'Excuse me, am I a heifer or a steer?' Ladies' loos may also, on a particularly bad day, be called 'Virgin Territory' or 'No Man's Land'. In some parts of the States, readers should also be alerted to lavatories with three doors marked 'His', 'Hers' and 'Don't Knows'.

In both countries the drawings that accompany – or worse, in some cases, replace – these inscriptions are almost without exception impenetrable, and must never be trusted, particularly in these days when the arbiters of high fashion decree the use of interchangeable clothing. For example, which door do you go through if, like a somewhat myopic Shea, you come face to face with two doors marked thus?

I give up! Both are doing a Highland fling, but neither is wearing a kilt....

In addition, any reader who encounters one of those hand-drying machines that does *not* switch off before the hands are dry is asked to contact the authors and recommended to buy shares in the manufacturing company. (Graffiti in a loo in Dallas, Texas, on one such machine: 'Press here for a message from your Senator.')

Whatever you call it, the relief facility is the place where you really come face to face with the writing on the wall, the people's prose. We thought of running a section comparing transatlantic standards, but material found by our team of researchers was almost universally considered to be too much for this happy family treatise. None the less, the following caught our attention:

Smile, you're on *Candid Camera*.

NEW YORK

Like a nice time, dearie? Dial 1 2 3.

EDINBURGH

IF YOU SEE AN UNATTENDED BAG ... *ask her if she'd like a nice time.*

LONDON

KINDLY ADJUST YOUR DRESS BEFORE LEAVING *since refusal often offends.*

LONDON

10
The Traveller's Survival Kit

"

One matter Englishmen don't think in the least funny is their happy consciousness of possessing a deep sense of humour.

MARSHALL MCLUHAN

Whatever else an American believes or disbelieves about himself, he is absolutely sure he has a sense of humour.

E. B. WHITE

Public telephones in Europe are like our pinball machines: they are primarily a form of entertainment and a test of skill rather than a means of communication.

Miss Piggy's Guide to Life

Americans are remorseless. They invite you to a party. You can't say, I've got a splitting headache – they'll send the doctor around.

V. S. PRITCHETT

"

The gentle British visitor arriving Stateside – especially via
New York, as most of them do – need not worry too much
about getting lost. There are always plenty of people about to
ask. Getting the answer you want is stage two. Thus:

'Excuse me, which way is Fifth Avenue?'
'I ain't no information kiosk.' Or:

'I say, I'd like to get to the Metropolitan Museum.'
'So? Who's stopping you?'

This sort of welcome is not universal, though it doubtless prompted the fifth Earl of Cadogan to advise: 'Don't go abroad. It's a dreadful place.' But presuming you've gone, there are ways of being prepared for coping with the States, and avoiding the worst. Here are some survival techniques.

THE BRITON IN AMERICA

THINGS THE BRITISH TRAVELLER NEED NOT WORRY ABOUT

- Getting Montezuma's Revenge. (He was Mexican. OK, so you can avoid US-Mexican restaurants.)

- Earthquakes. They don't happen too often in Maine, and you can always check the fault lines before you decide where else to go.

- Rattlesnakes, grizzly bears, muggers – if you've got a good comprehensive health insurance cover.

- Being thought rude. Unless you really work at it.

- The dollar/sterling exchange rate. (It's always bad.)
  Hooker: 'There's an Englishman in there. Get him out! Get him out!'
  Madame: 'English vice, eh? Sodomy and the lash? That's what he's after, eh?'
  Hooker: 'No – worse. He wants to pay in sterling.'

The locals you meet will want to forget about sterling. So should you. Continual attempts to work out how much things are costing you in pounds will rapidly drive you into a state akin to that in the first item on this list.

GETTING AROUND THE STATES

Avoid public transport unless you can't afford not to. (Especially the New York subway, remember). It is the country of the motor car and everything is geared to it. Some parts of some cities simply are not made for walking in, especially LA where only social outcasts walk. Elsewhere you may get arrested for even trying: tell them you're jogging if that happens. Otherwise, as Tom Lehrer might have said, if the muggers don't get you, the carbon monoxide will. (But anyway, note that signs saying 'ped Xing' don't refer to paedophiles or pederasts, but mark places where you can cross the road in some towns).

Driving makes it all different. Everything goes for the motorist; motorways, freeways, tollways, driveways, parkways, good signposting, good service areas, good campsites, rest stops, hamburger joints – even (once seen outside Dallas) a drive-in massage parlour.

If you have to ask the way, watch out for pronunciation changes. The street in Chicago named after the German philosopher Goethe emerged, following a request for directions, as Go-ethey Street.

THE LAW

'How much justice can you afford, Mr Smith?' was the caption of a famous *New Yorker* cartoon, by our own respected illustrator, no less. Thus also the view in Britain of American justice – thanks, as usual, to American television series. All Brits know that the only way a real American guy can get justice is to go out alone, preferably in the noonday sun, and take it with his own hands. In Britain, by contrast, the law is ponderous and boring.

Presuming, however, that no reader of this book can be classified as, or is proposing to become, a serious law-breaker, but on the other hand wishes to be alert to the minor dos and don'ts of the prevailing systems, what should be looked out for on a day-to-day basis?

Traffic laws If you step off the pavement (or rather, the sidewalk) and get knocked over, this may be because you forgot they drove on the wrong (right) side of the road. Result: you lose. Otherwise, traffic laws are excitingly different wherever you go from state to state, Can you turn right at a red light? Or is it left? Parking restrictions also vary, from minor fines to being wheel-clamped or towed away to a police stockade. Incidentally, in some States you can, automatically, go to jail if you don't have your driving licence with you. Be prepared to produce your passport as well, as British licences don't carry a photograph – and expect total disbelief when they realize that the licence's expiry date is sometime in the next century. They'll either cart you off to jail anyway, or hold you up for two hours while they reminisce about the six months they spent at Lakenheath while in the USAF. British police or traffic wardens can't fine you on the spot. In certain States everyone knows that the cops make their living that way. (And don't try to talk them out of giving you a ticket or it will only get worse.)

Licensing Laws If you get drunk and hit a cop the consequences of your action may well be much the same whichever side of the Atlantic you find yourself on. Some states require young people to carry a pass (or ID) before they can be given a drink in a pub or bar; some counties don't yet recognize the end of prohibition. You have been warned.

WHAT THE BRITISH TRAVELLER WILL MISS

One of the most important aspects of adjusting to a new life on the opposite side of the Atlantic concerns the negative, the absence, the lack, the things you won't find that you want to find. Such things are few and far between, and get fewer and fewer as transatlantic tastes gradually coincide. In any case, why lack anything when (at least if you are rich) you can import it? But, as you won't find much in the way of free medical services, take out maximum insurance cover against:

    rape
    pillage
    toothache
    mugging
    hurricanes
    athlete's foot
    Los Angeles air

If you have to be rushed to emergency, be prepared to pay before you get your blood transfusion.

THINGS THE BRITISH CAN PROBABLY DO WITHOUT

Currently on offer in the States to members of a society saturated by affluence are some items that have to be classed as strictly non-essential.

Even faced with the eccentricities of American hotel air-conditioning, you probably don't need, at $89.95, your own sleepmate. No, it's not an inflatable rubber doll but a battery-operated portable machinelet that 'electronically produces the sound of rainfall and waterfalls to mask out unwanted noises [presumably those of your air-conditioning, or the sounds of plumbing, quarrels and lovemaking] in your hotel or motel room'. It may also soothe you to sleep.

Massage beds that vibrate for a quarter in the slot are also available in many hotels. Worth trying if you want a preview of what an earthquake feels like before reaching California.

You may not crave your own personalized gearshift knob; still less a portable smoke-detector kit, unless you're in the habit of smoking in bed as you watch the coin-operated blue movies on your hotel room television. (Incidentally, on the latter, even some quite respectable hotels allow you to watch porn films by setting a special dial on your television set. You are then billed automatically when you check out the next day. Beware hotels that itemize everything including the name of the film, particularly if you're a member of a gospel revival convention and someone is going to scrutinize the bill. This also applies if you avail yourself of escort services that accept credit cards. Any Barclaycard statement that includes 'The House of Pain and Domination – $75' may be difficult to explain to your better half or your employer.) Off your shopping list are also portable hamburger warmers, safes that bolt on round the base of the loo, and of course your cowboy boot bag for keeping them in perfect antelope leather security. Then (an anti-marketing device for microwave cookers surely?) how about this ad: 'Don't get zapped by microwaves when radiation starts leaking as the seals go on your micro-oven. Keep you and yours safe.' And all for a mere $19.95. Then there are portable heartbeat, blood pressure and stress control monitors to measure all these strains that choosing your ultimate luxury will impose on you.

THE AMERICAN IN BRITAIN

GETTING AROUND

By and large, even the big British cities are safer than their counterparts in the States. Mugging is still relatively uncommon and the police are generally both helpful and unarmed. Public transport is reasonable and inexpensive – when it's not on strike.

Finding your way around can be tricky since there is less consistency in road direction signs, street signs and house numbering systems than in the United States. Spot the quaint warning signs: 'Hedgehogs crossing', 'Caution: Frogs migrating', etc. There are also some types of street that don't exist Stateside, e.g. 'Mews', which is a small lane behind the houses of a big street where you used to find the old coach houses and servants' quarters. Now they are universally converted into fashionable 'bijou residences' for fashionable people, particularly in London. Note also 'Gates' which aren't gates but roads, as in the Scottish 'gang yer ain gait' or 'gate'.

Watch when crossing streets. It takes at least a week to remember that traffic drives on the left. At traffic lights, cars turning left or right need not stop for pedestrians. Not even you.

THINGS THE AMERICAN TRAVELLER NEED NOT WORRY ABOUT

- Rattlesnakes
- Hurricanes
- The accuracy of stories in British tabloids
- Mugging – as opposed to begging
- Saying 'Thank you very much' a sufficient number of times in 30 seconds
- Having good enough manners – nothing will be good enough
- Sunburn
- Over-effective air conditioning
- Over-hasty service
- Over-strong coffee

WHAT THE AMERICAN TRAVELLER MAY FIND WANTING

Bathrooms God gave Britain a dank, moist climate. You'll find it in your typical British bathroom.

Central heating Check the small print before booking into that adorable little old-fashioned hotel, especially in winter. The same applies with rented apartments – and here, also remember that each British domestic appliance (washing machine, drier, etc.) has its own personality. It's all part of British individuality.

Ice Something, if available at all, that is hoarded in all hotels, pubs and restaurants, and issued reluctantly, one cube at a time.

Valet parking If you are used to moving from one subterranean parking area to another with the doors locked from the inside and only emerging in the light of day to relinquish your auto to a valet parker, forget it.

Flights (frequency of)   You'll envy Shea's experience in the States: 'Terribly sorry, Sir. Your flight [from Denver, Colorado to Sheridan, Wyoming – population 15,000] has been cancelled.' Groan, groan. 'Fortunately, Sir, we have a further flight in five minutes' time. I hope this won't inconvenience you? Have a nice day.' And don't expect somewhere to hang your hanging bag if you carry it on board a domestic British flight.

WEATHER

Let us say it out loud: the British (despite it being their greatest national fixation) are very lucky with their weather and, by extension, with their other natural elemental conditions too. Unlike the US of A, Britain is almost free from hurricanes, typhoons, desert heat, tornadoes, whirlwinds, real blizzards, floods and other mind-bending acts of God. By and large British weather is mild: never very warm, never very cold, never (in global terms) very windy, wet, dry, sunny, snowy or frosty. American visitors should plan for October all year round. And the buildings are but seldom shaken by earth tremors, never menaced by volcanic lava flows.

All of these come and go, courtesy of the hand of the Almighty, with annual regularity across the United States. You can bake on Third Avenue, New York at over 100°F and you can ski the length of it within the space of a few short months. You can be rattled like a ... rattle ... in Los Angeles, where they wait in perpetuity for the great disaster to end all disasters. Flooding and drought are commonplace. As usual, Mark Twain said it all:

> There is a sumptuous variety about the New England weather that compels the stranger's admiration – and regret. The weather is always doing something there; always attending strictly to business; always getting up new designs and trying them on the people to see how

they will go. But it gets through more business in spring than in any other season. In the spring I have counted one hundred and thirty-six different kinds of weather inside of four-and-twenty hours.

Mind you, the weather in Britain changes even quicker, if anything. It just is that it doesn't change so much.

MEDIA

A nation gets the media it deserves. So said someone, sometime. How true and how wise that cliché is. Again, the anonymous wise man said, the media only give the people what they want. Reporting styles and journalistic ethics are but a minor reflection of the society in which they live and move and invent their exclusives. What then of the British and American media scene? Is it true that the one country has wise television and foolish newspapers and the other vice versa?

THE BRITISH MEDIA

'Surely,' an American journalist of our acquaintance cried, 'the British do not deserve their press. It's rather below the sort of paper that's fit for puppy-dogs to play with.' He was talking about those Fleet Street tabloids whose headlines scream that this is the paper with everything – everything, that is, except news. Little has changed from Jane Austen's day:

> Lady Middleton exerted herself to ask Mr Palmer if there was any news in the paper.
> 'No, none at all,' he replied, and read on.

The end product is bingo, sex and a never-ending search for the lowest common denominator by or with which to entice

the reader. Note especially catch-all words like 'exclusive' (i.e., stories common to almost all the others), as well as 'fury', 'sex', 'anguish', 'boycott', 'shock', 'sex', 'horror', 'no-holds-barred', 'intimate', 'starlet', 'confirmed bachelor', 'drama', 'constant companion', 'exposé', 'frolic' 'old Etonian', 'revelation', 'orgy', 'vice', 'naughty', 'nights of passion', 'explicit', 'sensation' and 'Princess Di' (or just 'Di').

One advantage of going to the States is that you won't be able to find a Fleet Street tabloid (or any other British newspaper) until you're on the British Airways flight home. Except, that is, in supermarkets, where they masquerade as the *National Enquirer* and the *Star*.

As America kindly disposes of its old series to the old country, British television is very like American television except
that there is less of it. There is still a certain amount of British
content. Every American knows that all the best programmes
which appear in the United States are from the BBC, since
that's synonymous with British broadcasting. When British
independent television companies want to replace their top
management they send them to the States to hear that sort
of remark so that they become terminally ill with fury.

There is also much less advertising on British TV, which is
a GOOD THING – only seven minutes in every hour and
even then only on two of the four channels. Unlike the US,
where to the eyes of newly arrived British tourists there is
seven minutes of programming for every fifty-three minutes
of ads.

THE AMERICAN MEDIA

America has a great advantage over Britain, in that its national press isn't. (OK, OK, we know: the *Wall Street Journal*
and *USA Today*.) There are, however, many famous
metropolitan-based newspapers, some of them not owned yet
by Mr Rupert Murdoch and whose editors thereby are still
exempt from Mr Adlai Stevenson's remark: 'An editor is one
who separates the wheat from the chaff and prints the chaff.'

Any British visitor who arrives in America and switches on
the television set will be mystified by how many choices there
are and how little there is to watch. The Public Broadcasting
System (PBS) is the only supplier of 'quality' programming;
practically all of its dramatic series are imported from England; which is why Alistair Cooke seems to be its patron saint.
Generally, as the poor British viewing public know, a good

American television play, series, serial, etc., will live up to Sam Goldwyn's remark: 'We want a story that starts with an earthquake and works its way up to a climax.' Trouble is the stuff that one has to sit through on the way.

Generally, cable television has not lived up to its promise of supplying top-quality TV for every esoteric taste. Other than a twenty-four-hour news channel (Cable News Network – it's rather good) and the introduction of MTV (twenty-four hours of music videos) the rest of the shows look like throwback, amateur network television. However, Andy Warhol's dictum about everybody being famous for fifteen minutes seems to be coming true in 'public access' shows on local cable television systems; these allow any Joe and Harry to spend about $40 a week and put on the *Joe and Harry Show*. Local cable operators also offer sex shows; in New York, there is the *Nude Talk Show*, particularly distinctive for its camera work.

Another cable television innovation was a show hosted by Dr Ruth Westheimer called *Sexually Speaking*. Dr Westheimer was born in Poland and studied in Germany; she sounds like a Mel Brooks routine when she answers 'kvestions', her voice dipping up and down like a put-on of a Freudian analyst. She is, however, very earnest, and kind and sincere, and genuinely cares about her letter-writers and phone-callers; she gives smart advice, but beware: her forthrightness about saying things like, 'Do you put his penis in your armpit?' might put you off a bit.

The undisputed king of daytime TV is Phil Donahue. He's a sleek-looking guy who wears his white hair like an aggressive helmet. He's got the endurance of an Olympic athlete as he works his studio audience, running up and down steps, pushing his cordless microphone in people's faces. Meanwhile, the crowd loves it. Women love him for his feminism; he tries to fight for the poor and the oppressed and rails against 'the blue suits in their air-conditioned offices', forgetting that he often wears smartly tailored blue suits and charges around a freezing studio. His shows range in topics

from such obvious crowd-pleasers as 'Men in skirts' (he'll pick
out the most obviously conservative man in the audience and
hit him with 'Whaddya think, fella?') to a discussion of American Communism ('Would you be happier in Russia, huh?').
He wins many awards, and deserves them.

There are two syndicated shows not to be missed, falling
into the Made-in-California category.

One is *The People's Court*. Judge Wapner, a retired guy
who's cruel but fair, presides over small claims cases in which
the parties have agreed not only to settle out of court but to
settle on national television. Most of the cases involve put-out
drycleaners or re-upholsterers ('I told her she could expect it
to shrink, and then I offered to redo it') or angry neighbours.

The other, *Love Connection*, is the mid-eighties version of
The Dating Game, a silly seventies show in which 'bachelors'
and 'bachelorettes' selected each other, won chaperoned
dates, and then were never heard from again. Here, however,
with the use of modern technology, an available man or
woman selects his or her intended from videotapes (we see
excerpts) and then comes back to report the outcome of the
date in excruciating detail (and there are no chaperones, unlike Cilla Black's squeaky clean *Blind Date* on ITV). Sometimes
it works; in that case, the couple sits on the couch together
and giggle, 'No, she was the one who asked how I liked my
coffee in the morning.' If it was a dud, the two are seen on a
split screen, the offending parties in separate rooms. 'So he
came to pick me up, and I thought, "Oh no, another one
who's fat and forty."' 'Oh yeah?' he interjects. 'She had her
own little weight problem and then never shut up about her
job.' People used to do anything on American television for
a set of free Samsonite luggage; now they'll do anything on
American television for a moment on American television.

ADVERTISING

Early to bed and early to rise,
Work like hell, and advertise.

ANON.

American advertising is rarely as funny or clever as British advertising; although it is getting better, marketeers want to make sure you get the message and the product name, even if it means clubbing you over the head with it. When advertisers do come up with something successful, they tend to run it into the ground, as in 'Where's the Beef?' And since copywriters eat, drink and sleep advertising, they get a little carried away with their copy points, hence an advertisement for a yoghurt in which the announcer said: 'Greatness – you expect it in yourself, you demand it in your yoghurt!'

Women, who are still the prime buyers – consumer durables-wise – seem to get most of the attention in commercials these days. Men are there mostly to run the power mower or say that they prefer potatoes to rice. Or they are foils for marketeers trying to show how unsexist their commercials are: one laundry commercial shows a woman coming in the door with her slingback shoes and attaché case flying (standard issue for working women in commercials). After the 'Hey honey, I'm home' stuff, he starts telling her how he's cooked up duck à l'orange. But she notices the ring around his collar, and takes him by the ear down to the laundry room to show him how to do the laundry properly.

Also surprising to the British eye will be the willingness of former movie and TV stars to come forward and sell dentures or denture cream. One man stands there emitting a six-syllable 'Ooooooooooch' when he describes what it feels like to get seeds under your plate. Also, it is not uncommon to see people sitting around a table, as a moderator lists the problems they encounter with dentures: 'Stains, slippage, seeds.' US ads are for a notably greater range of products than are UK ads which concentrate on what to eat, drink and feed to your dog, cat or budgie. In America, don't be surprised, as you settle down to a late room-service snack, to be assaulted with commercials for cures for piles, 'intimate' deodorant sprays and remedies for 'jock' itch. On the other hand, entrepreneurial young companies like Nike (shoes) do produce genuinely good commercials.

MONEY

Wine maketh merry: but money answereth all things.

ECCLESIASTES 10:19

In the US, once you've learnt the jargon (nickel, dime, quarter, buck, grand, etc.) and the fact that no other currency exists except the dollar, you are home and dry.

The British money system has a few elephant traps to watch out for. There are a hundred pence (pennies) to the pound and coins of one, two, five, ten, twenty and fifty pence; the last two are seven-sided. The pound (sterling) comes both in note (i.e., bill) form – though this is being abolished except in Scotland where they issue their own bank notes – and as a thick, gold-coloured coin. Larger notes come in various denominations: five, ten, twenty and fifty. If you've been travelling in Scotland you needn't (legally speaking) off-load their notes before coming south, and you will have absolutely no trouble whatsoever in paying suspicious cab drivers with them, even if they are of large denomination. (But beware of *Irish* [Republic] money, which is not acceptable in Britain, even though the coins are of exactly the same sizes and denominations.)

The penny is called a 'pee', so be careful to differentiate between wanting a pee and wanting one pee, or spending a penny and spending a penny.

A SHORT COMPARATIVE TREATISE ON BRITISH AND AMERICAN SHOPPING

When the going gets tough, the tough go shopping.
ROBIN WILLIAMS

It's easier in the States, especially food shopping. Supermarkets become megastores, and the goodies are easily and rapidly transferred from well-stocked and displayed shelves to trolleys, past rapid-action cashiers (where someone actually packs your purchases into cartons or brown paper bags) and from thence to your car boot (sorry, trunk). Shops stay open longer; goods are sold in greater quantities (from soap powder to whisky); and the range of choice is wider. But you need bigger rubbish bags and tips to take away all the extraneous packaging in which even the most humble item is wrapped. (Somehow one large bag of groceries as bought will, when unpacked, produce half a bagful of actual contents and two full bags of jettisonable paper, cardboard, polystyrene, cellophane, plastic, padding, etc.) You won't find much of the old-fashioned personal touch in shopping which by reputation is meant to exist in Britain.

But when, oh British, did you last find that back home? Ah well. Reputation's one thing. And the Brits do still have Harrods and Fortnum & Mason, as well as the sweet little corner sweetshops now run by enterprising Pakistanis.

A SHORT TREATISE ON COMPARATIVE HUMOUR

Both British and Americans like to laugh at many of the same things – e.g., at politicians, who are always good for a laugh. Generally speaking, however, political cartooning is more developed and acerbic in the States while jokey-type jokes are more poignant and whimsical in the UK. Both countries support distinguished 'classic' funny magazines like *Punch* and the *New Yorker*, which the vast majority of the inhabitants of both countries don't find at all funny, perhaps, their editors believe, because they don't appreciate high-class intellectual satire. Try them and you'll see what we mean. In Britain, *Punch* is only found in dentists' waiting rooms, so much so that Michael Shea claims that reading it always gives him toothache.

A British Foreign Office manual of etiquette used to advise diplomats thus: beware the dangers of wit and the pitfalls of humour, especially when dealing with foreigners. Quite right. Comedy travels badly, as the famous British broadcaster, Gilbert Harding, found out in the 1950s when arriving in New York. Mr Harding, in common with other less well-known passengers, was required to fill in a long form for immigration officials which sought to establish, among other things, if the purpose of his visit was 'to overthrow the republic'. Mr Harding scribbled in the space provided: 'Not sole purpose of trip.' Moments later he was under arrest.

AMERICAN AND BRITISH HUMOUR
Stand-Up Comedy – Contrasting Styles

American

In opening, the American comic feels a need to ingratiate himself with the MC, the audience and the host city:

'Thank you for that kind introduction, Marty. Nice fellow. He sent a Rolls-Royce to the airport to pick me up. Which is kind of silly because I was at the Greyhound bus depot! Hey, it's great to see so many smiling faces. You look as though you found parking spaces! Hey, it's great to be back in Des Moines – it's one of my favorite cities. I spent a summer here once in '73 and it didn't snow once!'

Parking, since he mentioned it, is one of the American comic's obsessions:

'Saw a guy last week lying in the road. I said, "what's the matter – you fall over?" He said, "no, I just found this parking space so I've sent my wife out to buy a car!"'

British

While the British comic goes straight in with the first gag:

'Hasn't the weather been marvellous? Nice for the holidays. You been yet? We went in April – well, I like to get in early while the sheets are still clean!'

While the British comic's major obsession is with his mother-in-law:

'My mother-in-law's just got a new job – she works out at Heathrow, kick-starting Jumbos!'

Which leads him into another recurring theme, Japanese compact cars:

'Hey, what about these new Japanese compacts. Talk about small! I put my hand out to turn left the other day and one of them drove right up my sleeve!'

Most American routines embrace a joke or two about flying:

'Boy, they sure pack those passengers in on those planes today! I was in a Jumbo jet took off from New York last week with five hundred passengers. Ten minutes later it makes a forced landing at Newark with a hernia!'

If the joke fails to get a laugh, the American comic will say,

'I don't use a laugh track in this act. The silence you hear is absolutely genuine!'

Which leads him into another recurring theme, her cooking:

'She thinks she's a good cook. You should try her pastry! I'm not saying it's heavy, but she's the only woman in this street with a bow-legged gas stove!'

And most English ones, a joke or two about lazy workers – usually at British Leyland or Liverpool docks:

'So one worker says to the other, "I see the daffodils are out." So his mate says, "Are we coming out in sympathy?"'

While the British comic will say,

'Me English. . . .'

Which will attract the first heckle of the evening, which the American comic will deal with by saying,

'Why don't you go down to the morgue and tell them you're ready!'

Moving swiftly along, the American comic will use the name

'Akron, Ohio.'

... which is comedian's code for a dirty and unpleasant place in which no one would wish to live. He employs it in the following joke:

'Great place, Akron. You wake up in the morning and hear the birds outside coughing!'

Other comedians' code words for 'funny' places in America are

'Biloxi',
'Sheboygan'
and
'Burbank'.

While the English comic's retort will be:

'Why don't you follow the example of your head and come to the point!'

The English comic mentions

'Neasden.'

... with similar effect. The joke he tells goes like this:

'I first saw the light of day in Norwich. I was actually born two years earlier in Neasden!'

While the British comic resorts to

'Chipping Sodbury',
'Cleethorpes'
and
'Budleigh Salterton' (again).

Turning, for his last gag, to the world of sexual politics, the American comic chooses a 'gay' theme:

'Terrible thing happened when I was away from home last month. A marauding gang of gays broke in ... and redecorated my apartment!'

And so the closing routine, the traditional song. The title will be announced as:

'Careless Hands – or The Cry of the Wild Goose.'

But after inviting the piano player to

'... oblige with an arpeggio'

... the American comic will actually sing:

'My Way.'

And as the final bars play he will remember to flatter his audience one last time:

'Goodnight! Hey, you're beautiful! Thank you! Hey, I'd like to take you home with me! etc., etc.'

The British audience is not quite ready for that sort of sophistication. Better give them the old Women's Lib gags?

'My wife's got into this women's liberation. She decided to burn her bra. Trouble was, nobody told her she had to take it off first!'

The British comic will announce his intention of singing:

'Don't sit on the gas stove, Granny – you're too old to ride the range'

But after inviting the piano player to

'... start pedalling, Vicar'

... the British comic will actually sing:

'Please Release Me.'

And as the final bars play, his exit will be somewhat more brisk:

'I must go now – I've got a fair bit to do at the office! Thank you! Good night!'

Epilogue

Well, there it is. Britain revelling in its past, America revelling in its future. Britons tending to understate, Americans to overstate. Britons and Americans, because they speak the same language and share so many of the same habits, fondly believing they understand each other, when so much of the time they palpably don't.

However, for the non-xenophobic American visitor to Britain, surely you will have encountered little of the arrogance recommended by Cecil Rhodes when he said, 'Remember that you are an Englishman, and have consequently won first prize in the lottery of life.' You may even at times bemoan some of the self-doubt that has befallen the old Imperial self-confidence. Indeed you may have found, as Negley Farson did in 1949, 'You can do wonders with an Englishman if you make him feel ashamed of himself.' Certainly, as we have hinted, you cannot have discovered the same situation as George Orwell did in 1941: 'England is the most class-ridden country under the sun. it is a land of snobbery and privilege, ruled largely by the old and silly.'

With luck you will have found quirkiness and eccentricity as Bob Hope did: 'The place was so English, I wouldn't have been surprised if the mice wore monocles.' And indeed a quirky and eccentric difference of values similar to that which Somerset Maugham observed: 'American women expect to find in their husbands the perfection that English women only hope to find in their butlers.' Perhaps your conclusions will bear some similarity to those of George Santayana: 'England is not ... the best possible world but it is the best actual country, and a great rest after America.' You may not agree with the first half of the sentence, but we hope that you will have found it a great rest. (Back in 1922, incidentally, Santayana also described England as 'the Paradise of individuality, eccentricity, heresy, anomalies, hobbies and humours'.)

If you are one of our British readers visiting America, you may have come upon the comment of Arnold Toynbee when he said, 'America is a large friendly dog in a small room. Every time it wags its tail, it knocks over a chair.' That has quite a lot to say about America's role in the world, but the word 'friendly' is central to the experience of any visitor arriving in America. Americans do very much want to be loved. As Lance Morrow said, 'It bewilders Americans to be hated.' Perhaps thas why Americans are such notable exponents of euphemism. Years ago Evelyn Waugh wrote to Nancy Mitford: 'American polite vocabulary is very different from ours. We fight shy of abbreviations and euphemisms. They rejoice in them. The blind and maimed are called 'visually/physically challenged', while the destitute are 'socio-economically confronted'. Much more recently, John Kenneth Galbraith took up the same theme: 'A physician, at least in the United States, does not tell you that a patient is dying. He says that the prognosis as of this time is without significant areas of encouragement.' And the authors were delighted to find the National Transportation Safety Board continuing the tradition as recently as 1984 when it described plane crashes as 'controlled flights into terrain'.

Americans are a good deal more concerned about youth than their British counterparts, who indeed seem distressingly immune even to the recent record levels of youth unemployment. As Malcolm Muggeridge commented, 'The pursuit of happiness, which American citizens are obliged to undertake, tends to involve them in trying to perpetuate the moods, tastes and aptitudes of youth.' In the words of an earlier traveller, the Duke of Windsor, 'The thing that impresses me most about America is the way parents obey their children.'

Americans want their children – and everyone else – to be happy. As John Updike said, 'America is a vast conspiracy to make you happy.' Or as Mary McCarthy put it, 'The happy ending is our national belief.'

May all your Mid-Atlantic wanderings have just such a happy ending.